9 00/H

SZIGETI
on the
VIOLIN

SZIGETI, Joseph. Szigeti on the violin. Praeger, 1970 (c1969). 234p il 71-95361. 11.00

CHOICE   MAY '71

Music

This book will attract the professional musician, notably string players, rather than the lay music lover. Although there is much of general
interest to the latter in part one of the book, part two is confined to
highly technical aspects of playing the violin. As a textbook for the
violinist, the work is excellent. Szigeti is a recognized master of his
instrument, and the advice he offers on intonation, fingering, bowing,
vibrato, tone coloration, as well as things purely musical, is invaluable.
His comments regarding the supply of string players for the modern
symphony orchestras may serve as a warning that time is running out,
and that we may witness the demise of the symphony concert before
the century ends. Although his style of writing does not flow easily,
and is often cumbersome, what he has to say more than compensates
for lack of readability.

196

By the same author

With Strings Attached
A Violinist's Notebook (Duckworth)

JOSEPH SZIGETI

SZIGETI
on the
VIOLIN

CASSELL · LONDON

CASSELL & COMPANY LTD
35 Red Lion Square, London WC1
Melbourne, Sydney, Toronto
Johannesburg, Auckland

© Joseph Szigeti 1969
First published 1969
S.B.N. 304 93471 2

Printed in Great Britain by
The Camelot Press Ltd., London and Southampton
F.669

CONTENTS

page

Introduction   ix

Part I

1   Is concerned mainly with the Then and the Now and the beginning of the Author's *Lehrjahre*   3

2   Recalls the Queens Hall, Henry Wood, Busoni, Beecham and many others and tells how long it was before the author tackled the Beethoven Concerto. A long tour and an enforced stay in a sanatorium   6

3   Extends the formula of the Then and the Now to the institution of the recital: from the last third of the nineteenth century to the last third of the twentieth century   9

4   Continues the foregoing by speculating on the recital's chances of survival in the twenty-first century and touches upon the emergence in our own times of the game of chance called 'Competition'   13

5   Glances at the interaction of competitions with the gramophone industry and contrasts the slow maturing of the virtuosi of former generations (in orchestral and teaching posts) with the mushroom-growth of careers in our time   18

6   An over-ambitious attempt to compress into far too few pages alarming data about the paucity of string players for orchestras in England, the United States, Germany and France   21

7   Speculates on the reasons for this state of things, questions whether the tuition right from the early stages onwards is at fault and, in addition, offers some case histories that may help to explain generalities (just as statistical data may help to clarify case histories)   27

8 Begins with a dictum of Carl Flesch about the importance of the orchestral player in the state of music in general and about the sins of omission and commission of teachers which in turn leads into saddening data concerning quacks, spurious claims and the like   33

9 Mainly about a didactic publication that—on the contrary—makes no such claims but proceeds serenely on its honest, musically health-giving course   38

10 An unsuccessful attempt to sum up, and an admission that a computer could do this better   42

Part II

11 Examines the question whether a change of string is more acceptable on a semitone or on a whole tone   47

12 Stresses the importance of tone colour, that is, the need to respect the composer's directions as to the string to be used, even at the price of discomfort. Hence to some examples where the exact opposite is suggested: namely the use of open strings for the sake of comfort!   52

13 Tries to dissuade violinists from playing identical repeated notes with the same finger by giving numerous examples from Beethoven, Mozart, Mendelssohn, Max Bruch, César Franck and others   58

14 Discusses the reasons for the neglect of a work like Schumann's A minor Sonata and incidentally censures music publishers for reprinting inadequate editions of eighty years and more ago. It also suggests that we sing, hum, whistle in a better tempo than we play   65

15 Demonstrates the advantages of an 'open' left hand after an excursion into elementary pedagogics quite unbecoming to a book of this kind but illustrated by digressions that range from Kreutzer to Bartók and Hindemith   70

16 Draws attention to the emancipation we owe to fingered octaves, mentions in passing the 'Geminiani grip' and Bartók's pattern of fourths, harks back to Chapter 12 *à propos* of tone colour and the judicious choice of strings, speaks about so-called crab-fingerings and ends—unexpectedly—on a hopeful note   80

17 Outlines the author's suggestion for overcoming an intonation pitfall   90

18 Devoted to Bach, and thus the core of the book; just as Bach should be the core of a violinist's life . . .   98

19 Follows the changes in our appreciation of the unaccompanied sonatas and partitas over the last hundred years   123

20 Some Bach misprints; and some others   127

21 Questions whether the uncertainties caused by the disagreement of editors are not sometimes responsible for the neglect of certain compositions. Liberties taken by editors with Tartini, Corelli, Handel   136

22 Examines some more textual problems—and Beethoven's changes of mind in the Violin Concerto   143

23 Pleads for respectful adherence to Debussy's precise demands for—momentarily unfashionable—slides between narrow intervals and incidentally touches upon related subjects   150

24 Brings into the open certain rhythmic and tempo distortions which we tacitly admit and condone   157

25 Probes the reasons why a simple um-tata accompaniment figure in Beethoven is difficult   166

26 Comments on the present disinclination to use open strings and deplores the lack of concrete describable facts about the playing of great figures like Joachim, Sarasate and others and brings together the little the author has gathered about some of these   168

27 Gives a glimpse of how critically and with what reluctance the *vibrato*—now indispensable—was regarded around the middle of the nineteenth century, and supplements the preceding chapter with some impressions of Joachim's playing   173

28 Concerns a bowing device variously called *'reprise de l'archet'*, the 're-taking' of the bow, and by other names, which enhances the speaking quality of certain phrase fragments   177

29 In which the author tries his hand at a definition of what he means by 'enhancement', incidentally invoking memories of Ysaÿe and Kreisler   181

30 Gives examples of other enhancements to show what can be done to attain a fuller realization of the composer's implied intentions that cannot always be defined in the printed page   184

31 More of the same, but with particular emphasis on bowing problems 190

32 Still more pages on the inexhaustible subject of bowing mastery, with some examples of bowings that are generally supposed to 'go against the grain' 197

33 Discusses clockwise and counter-clockwise bowing and touches upon those other endless subjects: bow articulation and fingerings 204

34 Speculates upon the decline in the use by teachers and students of variations such as those of Tartini and Paganini, written with a didactic aim. Concludes that they cannot be safely dispensed with 212

35 In the main a plea for the use of that violinist's treasury, Bartók's forty-four Violin Duets, incidentally discussing the ever-present matter of articulation in fragments in the Bartók Second Concerto, in Mendelssohn, Weber, Prokofiev, Bach, the 'Eroica', and Brahms 216

36 Conclusion 226

Index 228

INTRODUCTION

I HAVE tried in this book to do two things: first, to set down my thoughts about violinists and violin-playing in the contemporary musical scene from the point of view of one whose experience as student, child performer, international violinist, teacher, competition judge spans the greater part of the twentieth century; and secondly to pass on advice and suggestions that may help the violinist with his practical problems.

While writing the pages that follow I have often been haunted by the spectre of The Reader Who Bought This Book For The Wrong Reasons. He or she may have hoped for inspirational messages or else for infallible technical formulae, for 'short cuts', newly discovered 'secrets', the explanation of 'one of the most subtle violinistic mysteries—the closed violinistic circle' (I am quoting from a book published in 1961; the author writes that he is alluding to the 'picture' of left hand in a high position on the fingerboard, right hand holding the bow at the nut, the two hands near each other, creating practically a circle compounded of 'nape of the neck—shoulders—arms—hands').

All this is denied to my reader and what I am offering in the second half of this book is something very different.

I believe that what was acceptable in the way of inspirational messages forty or fifty years ago would be embarrassing to the student today. To give myself a warning example, I keep near at hand an edition of one of our masterworks by a greatly respected musician of those days in the Preface of which the words artist, musician, creators, bow art, soul, human body, equilibrium, sentiments, aspirations, human being, soul of the bow are all spelt with capital letters. Any reader who feels disappointed with what he finds here has only to adorn these key-words with capital letters in order to devise his or her own inspirational preface to pages in which such down-to-earth matters will be discussed as: 'change of string on a semitone versus change on a whole tone', 'change of finger on identical notes that are repeated', 'counter-clockwise bowings', '*reprise* of the bow', and many, many others.

It is likely that the reader whose spectre has been haunting me will find that I am stressing too many minor points, in fact, *trivia* (or rather, what *he* considers such). To him I would point out that in our craft it is often our fingerings, bowings, our manner of pointing up rhythmic aspects of the work, our individual tone and our way of singing a tune, the meaningful articulation of a phrase or a passage, that constitute our unmistakable 'handwriting', as his characteristic brushstroke sets a painter apart from others of his century or his school or period. And this is the one thing that seems to many observers to be lacking in our present crop of extremely brilliant violinists, the average of whose performing prowess is undoubtedly higher than it was a few decades ago.

I would be contradicting myself if I were to present ready-made solutions to the problems that I meet in my commerce with the masterworks. What I am hoping is that some of my experiments will stimulate students to experiment on their own and lead them to solutions that will be in their own 'handwriting'.

Let the reader then pick out of the pages that follow, out of this miscellany of suggestions, of advice, of criticism, whatever seems to apply to himself.

Let him be guided by the feeling that a finger is being pointed at him, personally, at his playing, at his lack of discrimination, lack of selectiveness, at whatever his particular 'lack' may be.

Let him forge his own style and adopt, or reject, mull over or criticize, but above all establish a dialogue between the book and himself.

Should the reader find that the question of intonation, the basic and all-important question in our art, is conspicuous by its absence in these pages, I would disculpate myself with one single sentence—a slogan, if you like—one that I borrow from an advertisement for a brand of mattresses in America: 'There Is No Substitute For Sleep. Buy X's Beauty-Rest Mattresses'. Applied to the subject of our book it would turn out less terse: 'There Is No Substitute For Perfect Intonation'.

Beauty of tone, perfection of technique, sense of style, the faculty of transmitting the essence, the poetry, the passion of a musical composition, all these gifts will be of no avail if the cardinal virtue of perfect intonation is missing. So let me repeat:

There Is No Substitute For Perfect Intonation.

Part I

CHAPTER 1

IS CONCERNED MAINLY WITH THE THEN
and the Now and the beginning of the
Author's Lehrjahre

THE TURN of the century, with which my *Lehrjahre* coincided, saw changes of every kind for the violin, as it did in so many other ways. There was the emergence of the Sevčik method and its star exponent Kubelik (b. 1880); rumours of the Auer school in St Petersburg and its products Elman (b. 1891) and Heifetz (b. 1901); and in my own Budapest was not Hubay's pupil Franz von Vecsey (b. 1893) a promise of things to come?

The solo concert as we know it, however, was only beginning to grow up; and its repertoire, still in the process of shedding the remains of the nineteenth-century ballad and Paganini–Liszt type of concert, had hardly begun to explore the riches which today are available to every student and amateur in three or four competing versions on gramophone records and also through broadcasting. Thus Vecsey's contributions to a concert in Budapest in 1903 consisted of Vieuxtemps' Concerto in E major, Wieniawski's 'Faust' Fantasy and Valse Caprice, Merkler's Berceuse and Hubay's Zephyr. I shall have more to say about the changes that have taken place in the recent repertoire in Chapter 3.

Without some idea of this background young players of today, with more methodical training and the benefits of gramophone and radio, might put down my late awakening entirely to my indolence . . . lethargy . . . call it what you will. One cannot, without over-simplification, ascribe it to any one cause.

My studies with Jeno Hubay lasted for only two school years, from 1903, when I was not yet eleven, to 1905, when I made my formal début in Berlin; for all parents of talented children in those days were impatient to enter them for the infant-prodigy race, and this made any long-range

3

teaching plans illusory. So it was not surprising that my master had to be content with getting me through a shortened course on the plan normally followed at that time, which encompassed a representative work of the Viotti–Kreutzer type (in my case the lovely A minor Concerto by Viotti—a favourite of Brahms's), then some Vieuxtemps, Wieniawski, the Ernst F sharp minor Concerto, Hubay's own virtuoso pieces and so on till we reach the Mendelssohn Concerto, the G minor by Max Bruch, the Bach Chaconne, E major Prelude and Gavotte, some Paganini—and with this repertoire the fathers of our *entourage* in those days felt justified in letting their offspring face the world in all their musical immaturity! I made my début in Berlin with the following three works: the Ernst Concerto, the Chaconne, and Paganini's Witches' Dance—rather a redoubtable choice and one obviously calculated to disarm rather than to please.

Small wonder then that it was only in my middle teens that I started to fill the lacunae in my musical equipment and began thinking of Beethoven, Brahms, Tchaikovsky, Lalo, Saint-Saëns, and Goldmark; that I took some lessons in harmony with Frederick Corder in London; and benefited from Hubay's extraordinary flair and suggestive power during some summer weeks spent with him in Ostend or at his summer residence in Hungary. During the winter months of concerts, when I was taking the line of least resistance in matters of repertoire, my practising was disordered and un-balanced. For the benefit of teachers and students I will give some details at the risk of seeming to focus attention unduly on my particular case, which is, after all, an untypical one. The duration, which I timed and noted down in the manner of an unwilling schoolboy, ranged from 135 to some 185 or 190 minutes;* and a typical work-plan was the Bach Prelude in E and a Paganini Caprice (probably 'La Chasse'), or else some Vieuxtemps Etudes and the *moto perpetuo*-type Presto from Sinding's A minor Suite, and forty-five minutes for scales.

Two short summer periods in 1908 spent near Hubay's château in Hungary (less than six weeks altogether) give a glimpse of the studious interludes which were a corrective to this way of working. The pieces I worked at and played for him were: the 'Kreutzer' Sonata, the Saint-Saëns Concerto, the Sinding Suite, the Goldmark Concerto, the Bach Chaconne and G minor Sonata and movements from the other sonatas, the

* Leopold Auer used to tell pupils: 'Practise three hours a day if you are any good, four if you are a little stupid. If you need more than that—stop. You should try another profession.'

Brahms Concerto, Hubay's Concerto No. II, Wieniawski's 'Faust' Fantasy, Hubay's Concerto *all' Antica,* the César Franck Sonata, Hubay's *Scène de la Csarda* No. II, the Bach Double Concerto, Corelli's La Follía, and Tartini's Devil's Trill. I also nibbled at the Beethoven Romances, and the Spring and the C minor Sonatas. When on my own, soon after these salutary few weeks, I diversified this material with sundry operatic Fantasias, Faust or Carmen, the Rondo Capriccioso by Saint-Saëns, some Sarasate, Hubay's Variations, Anton Rubinstein's Romance, and tackled Mozart's A major Concerto in a tentative and aimless way. These interludes, sporadic though they were, counterbalanced to a certain extent the lack of challenge in my professional activities which still centred round the same Tchaikovsky Concerto (first movement) and the same Wieniawski, Sarasate, Hubay pieces at the round of concerts in the provinces and Edwardian 'at homes' with Victorian programmes. Retarded, adolescent, all this seems to me today, when youngsters start their lives with imposing musical 'luggage' and take Bach C major Fugues, Alban Berg Concertos, Bartók solo Sonatas, Elgar and Sibelius Concertos in their stride— although this doesn't exclude some rather surprising let-downs, when they give us a Khatchaturian that is so immeasurably superior to their Mendelssohn. To understand the lack of challenge in my early years we have to envisage those years without broadcasting, without instrumental recordings worthy of the name, without competitions as we know them today.

Broadcasting, recordings, competitions keep our teenagers on the alert and aware of what their opposite numbers are doing. They keep a healthy competitive spirit alive; and what is being achieved in the classrooms of the Juilliard in New York, at the Moscow Conservatoire, in Paris or Brussels is common knowledge. It is not easy to harbour illusions. The competitions of which we have a surfeit nowadays keep those who follow them, either as entrants in the race or as listeners, on their toes; and this advantage somehow counterbalances the many negative aspects of this proliferating institution.

My own awareness of other young violinists was limited to Mischa Elman, to my countryman Vecsey, whom, however, I only rarely heard as he seldom played in England, and to some Auer pupils of approximately my age, such as the Canadian Kathleen Parlow, May Harrison and perhaps one or two others. It was easy to live in a fool's paradise in those days.

CHAPTER 2

RECALLS THE QUEEN'S HALL,
Henry Wood, Busoni, Beecham and many others and tells
how long it was before the Author tackled the Beethoven
Concerto. A long tour and an enforced stay in a sanatorium

QUEEN'S HALL was for my teenage years schoolroom and mountain top, from which I viewed great expanses of music. Henry Wood, then in the full *élan* of his admirable crusading spirit, Ysaÿe, Busoni, Kreisler, Mischa Elman—in comparison to me, imposingly mature—young Mr Beecham, Nikisch, Hamilton Harty accompanying Thibaud, coaching me in his D minor Concerto, these were my real teachers.

In those barren years, when I was no more than marking time, how salutary it was for me to be told by Thomas Beecham, during a rehearsal of the Bach E major Concerto, that the tempi of *allegros* in Bach's time had been brisker than I was inclined to take them. It was in 1907, at a rehearsal for one of Beecham's earliest concerts, but he radiated authority far beyond his years. He must have been entirely in the right. It is probable that my *allegro* tempo *was* on the stodgy side—'Victorian organist's Bach'.

Myra Hess, with whom I played Beethoven's C minor Sonata in Dundee in 1908, although my senior by barely two years, possessed a musical maturity and authority that was immensely imposing to a boy who was just then adding pieces like Sinding's Suite and Saint-Saëns' B minor Concerto to his repertoire and was generally still playing the Carmen Fantasies and Sarasate dances of his first programmes at joint recitals, ballad concerts and musical 'at homes'. It was Myra Hess, too, who initiated me into the Brahms D minor Sonata.

The one indication of my levelheadedness in those years seems to me now, as I look through old diaries and scrapbooks, the fact that I held the Beethoven Concerto in healthy respect; although I studied it from time to

6

time I did not attempt to play it in public until 9 December 1910, when I played it with the Stock Exchange Amateur Orchestral Society in London. I had just turned eighteen. My fee for this performance was five gold sovereigns enclosed in one of those golden containers with a spring from which one extracted one coin at a time. (Something like the gadget bus conductors use nowadays for small change.) And it is a good sign that the words BEETHOVEN CONCERTO appear in capital letters in my diary for that day. I did not tackle the Brahms Concerto either until I had reached the age of nineteen or twenty.

I find entries in my diaries like: 'Kreutzer Sonata, Kreutzer Etudes' when I was already seventeen or eighteen. The Kreutzer Etudes were a key influence in the formation of my equipment. They are considered by some nowadays as a stepping-stone that one uses but can later afford to discard. I see this when finished *virtuosi* and prize-winners at international competitions come to consult me. When I suggest that they play one of these *études* from memory and improvise one of the innumerable variants that every violinist should be able to invent for himself when he encounters some difficulty in one of the masterpieces, old or contemporary, there is a blank look on their faces. To them 'Kreutzer' means something long forgotten in their past.

But when, in the 1930s, while taking the cure in an Austrian spa, I dropped in on Arnold Rosé, an old master, Mahler's concertmaster and one of the great quartet leaders of the turn of the century, I found him with the Kreutzer Etudes propped up before him on the mantelpiece, practising them. At that time he was well over seventy.

That I continued to use the Kreutzer Etudes of my childhood as a springboard for technical devices of my own invention at a time when I already had several tours—Germany, Holland, France—to my credit indicates an artisan's willingness to work *in depth*. Today, when much that is being recorded is prepared by our enterprising young *virtuosi* at the behest of the equally enterprising 'artists and repertoire' men of the recording companies, in a minimum of time, before the works have been absorbed into the players' bloodstream, this is something that should be pondered.

There is little point in pursuing the gradual building-up of my musical equipment any further, now that the turning point, as I may call it, the Beethoven Concerto, has been reached. That it was reached in modest outward circumstances, with an amateur group, may have been all to the good and was somehow in tune with my timid approach to tasks which were new to me. Only recently I was told by friends of Sir Thomas Beecham how amused he was when, after our recording of the Mozart D major K. 218, he suggested our playing and recording the A major together and I replied: 'Oh no! Not yet . . .' This was in the 1930s and in fact quite some time elapsed before I added the A major to my repertoire. George Szell recently said that he wouldn't have dared to perform the Mozart G minor before he was forty years old. This diffidence in shouldering new musical responsibilities had a positive side to it. As I see it now, it may have been linked to my propensity for working in depth. For instance, I never played in public more than five of Paganini's twenty-four Caprices, but I perfected these to the point that I could face gramophone recording at a time when no corrections, no tape splicings were possible.

My diffidence, however, also made me miss many opportunities. When Kreisler gave the *première* of the Elgar Concerto in 1910, a *première* that created a stir such as we cannot visualize today, there I sat among the rapt audience, pencil poised above the music on my lap, trying to seize the '*insaisissable*' of Kreisler's eloquence, making notes . . . and yet I did *not* have the stamina to start work on it next day.

This is an humiliating admission to make when one considers that Eugène Ysaÿe, then in his fifties and not easily swayed to study a new work of such imposing dimensions and such demanding character, *did* undertake the first Berlin performance of the Elgar in 1912, which, according to Ysaÿe's letter to his wife, was '*une victoire pour l'œuvre et une grande joie pour l'interprète*'.

It would lead too far to try to describe the changes in my repertoire from about my twentieth year on. The Brahms, Beethoven, Busoni Concertos, the Brahms Sonatas, took the place in my activities which they should by rights have occupied much sooner. My tours ranged as far as Portugal and Finland, when suddenly a lung condition forced on me a prolonged stay in a sanatorium and my daily practice time was reduced to thirty or forty minutes!

The ingenuity I had to expend in order to draw the fullest dividends for the maintenance of my technique from these mere minutes has marked my practising methods right up to this day.

CHAPTER 3

EXTENDS THE FORMULA OF THE THEN
and the Now to the institution of the Recital: from the
last third of the nineteenth century to the last third of the
twentieth century

IT MAY PERHAPS help to bring out the differences between what I have
called the Then and the Now if we take a good look at the concert or
recital, as an institution, as it was some forty years before I started playing
in concerts. We are apt to think of this institution as something that has
always been with us and to forget how recently it attained its present form.

The programmes of the centenarian *Società del Quartetto* of Milan will
probably serve as well as any other set of programmes to trace this development. In Italy, the land of opera, instrumental chamber music had a harder
struggle than anywhere else to reach an audience. This is my reason for
choosing it as my point of departure; to have taken, say, London's St
James's Hall concerts would have made this necessarily brief description
less clear-cut and intelligible. For Joachim had already been a yearly visitor
to London since about 1849, and this, as well as other similar factors,
carries implications which need not be gone into here.

Italy in the last third of the nineteenth century was just beginning to
appreciate the chamber music and solo works which were the mainstay of
our music societies. The *Società del Quartetto* was founded by Verdi's
publisher, Tito Ricordi, in 1864; and at that time, as its historian, Giulio
Confalonieri, writes, 'A sonata, a quartet or a septet had never been heard
in its entirety in a concert or at a musical entertainment.' The days of
Paganini's legendary concerts with their 'Maestoso Sonata Sentimentale'
(*sic*), incorporating Haydn's 'Hymn to the Emperor' and 'St Patrick's Day'
(executed on the fourth string) and 'Carnival of Venice' Variations plus
'Farmyard Imitations' were not so far off, a mere thirty-five years. So it is

9

not surprising to see young Fritz Kreisler, aged twenty, offering the following programme in 1895: Handel's Sonata in A accompanied on the organ, followed by the Bach Chaconne, and rounding it off with the Cavatina from the Op. 132 Beethoven Quartet (!), pieces by F. Ries (of *Moto Perpetuo* fame, if fame it can be called), the Handel *Largo,* the Bach Gavotte in E and Paganini's *Moto Perpetuo.*

About the same time, in 1896, Busoni played in the same society, where orchestra and solo numbers used to alternate, an immeasurably more mature programme: the Beethoven G major Concerto, a Bach Prelude and Fugue, a Chopin Impromptu, the Schumann Toccata, Liszt's St Francis Legend and Polonaise in E. Sarasate's orchestra-accompanied programme in 1898 was made up of the Saint-Saëns and the Max Bruch Concertos, a Chopin Nocturne and some of his own Spanish Dances.

The renowned Emile Sauret (who later taught at the Royal Academy in London) solved his problem in 1899 by playing the Schumann D minor Sonata, a praiseworthy thought, considered by itself, but he followed it by the Beethoven Concerto, *accompanied on the piano,* a *Romanze* by Max Bruch and the Saint-Saëns *Rondo Capriccioso.* The piano-accompanied Beethoven Concerto caught the subscribers' fancy to such an extent that he opened his second concert with its first movement, following it with Vieuxtemps' A minor Concerto, a *Fantasia* by one Gernsheim and two *morceaux de salon* of his own confection.

But let us continue in less detail and get a bird's-eye view of the repertoire of the representative concert of the time (for this society, as we shall see, called upon the greatest names).

Joachim's choice for three concerts in 1880 is of a note-worthy *tenue.* For the first, a Haydn and a Beethoven quartet (probably played with local musicians), the Bach Chaconne and Schumann's A minor Sonata. The second programme: Spohr's Concerto VIII, Tartini G minor, Schumann's *Phantasie,* the Andante from his Hungarian Concerto and the third Brahms Hungarian Dance. Max Bruch's G minor and the Mendelssohn Concerto, the F major Romance of Beethoven and a Bach Solo Sonata made up the third programme. One of Sarasate's 1882 programmes was a curious mixture of quartet and solo numbers: Beethoven's C major (Rasumowsky) Quartet and the Andante from Schubert's A minor, probably played by the local quartet, the Variations from the 'Kreutzer' and *Zigeunerweisen* contributed by Sarasate.

From such a programme it is easy to imagine the 'split personality' of this subscription audience. Four years before, in 1878, Wilhelmj played the 'Kreutzer' Variations and the Bach Chaconne, both obviously favourites with the subscribers; the pianist gave the Anton Rubinstein Sonata and a Chopin Valse, a singer sang some Massenet and the quartet played Svendsen's Op. 1. In 1909 Ysaÿe and Kreisler played the same Viotti A minor Concerto at a distance of eleven days. Ysaÿe had already played it in 1889 in this society.

The year 1922 brought interesting contrasts with these 'prehistoric' programmes. The Budapest Quartet played Mozart, Haydn, Dittersdorf, Mendelssohn, Smetana, Dvořák, Pizzetti, Sgambati, Sinigaglia, Reger, Debussy but no Beethoven. The fine Australian violinist, Alma Moodie, little known outside Germany, offered Tartini, Nardini, short pieces by Bach and Beethoven, Lalo, Sinding, Schumann, Dvořák, Saint-Saëns, Wieniawski, Szymanowski in two concerts. Carl Flesch in his two programmes played Paganini and the whole G minor Sonata of Bach, a Reger Solo Sonata, Nardini, Locatelli, Saint-Saëns, Suk and Brahms Dances.

In 1942 a violin programme contained a Reger Suite, Bach A minor Adagio and Fugue, a Mozart and a Brahms Sonata and three pieces; in 1943 Gioconda De Vito gave three great works: the Schumann D minor, Beethoven C minor and the Devil's Trill.

Vasa Prihoda was courageous enough to play in 1947 the C major Adagio and Fugue by Bach, Schubert's Fantaisie Op. 159, Brahms' Op. 108 and Paganini. My programme shortly after was the Bach G minor Sonata, Busoni's second Sonata, the Debussy and two small pieces. Arthur Grumiaux played Veracini, Bach, Prokofiev and Stravinsky. The post-war years show the programme pattern as we know it now. The solo concert has come of age; it no longer takes courage, even in Italy, to offer a Beethoven Sonata, a Bach Solo Sonata and Schubert's Op. 159, or the Brahms Op. 78, the 'Spring' Sonata and the Ernst Bloch, as Isaac Stern did in 1958; the two Prokofiev Sonatas and the Stravinsky Divertimento are played quite often by different performers; Schubert's Op. 159 seems to have been accepted into the repertoire.

Eight programmes were played by the same violinist over twenty-five seasons (1927–46) in this society. One might expect that these would yield interesting data, especially as they were given by an artist with the strong stylistic profile of Bronislav Huberman, whose highly individual style of playing gave rise to controversy even after he had passed away (see Appendix to the *Memoirs of Carl Flesch*: Rockliff). But the overall yield of these eight programmes turns out to be rather disappointing. We find three performances each of the Bach Chaconne and the 'Kreutzer' Sonata, two each of the César Franck, the Handel D major, the Devil's Trill, the Mendelssohn Concerto and Brahms G major, one of the A major and, curiously enough, none of the D minor. Bach is represented by the B minor Partita, the Adagio and Fugue in C and the G minor Sonata, Beethoven by the two Romances and the Op. 96. Hindemith's early Op. 11, Sonatas by Respighi and Wolf Ferrari, Concertos by Tchaikovsky and Saint-Saëns and many Chopin and Schubert transcriptions, as well as several pieces by Szymanowski, Smetana, Wladigeroff and Sarasate complete these eight programmes.

There is no denying the solidity with which these eight programmes were built, yet one cannot avoid feeling that there is something static about them, spanning as they do a quarter of a century, and that too much consideration is shown for a public which not only 'knows what it likes' but which rather 'likes what it knows'.

Some curious omissions are also to be found in this society's activities, of which I have given a rapid glimpse; and these are probably also to be explained by the attitude of committees which cater for their members and give exaggerated consideration to the likes and dislikes of some of their subscribers. For instance, I have searched in vain in the index for the names of Béla Bartók and Serge Prokofiev, two pianist-composers who by rights should have been asked to give programmes of standard works with a generous sprinkling of their own compositions in the 1920s and 1930s when both were active on the concert platform. Such omissions have to be mentioned in the context of these pages for there is an interdependence between an artist's repertoire and the programme policy and attitude of those who direct the destinies of concert societies. In the long run the artist *does* react to what is manifestly wanted and what is not wanted by committees, managers and—in the last analysis—the public.

And so we end this chapter more hopefully, looking forward to a time when Mozart Sonatas other than the two in B flat major will be played, when Beethoven's even-numbered Sonatas will compete with the 'Kreutzer' and 'Spring', when Bartók's Second Sonata, Hindemith's Solo Sonatas, Schubert's Op. 162, will take their rightful place in the repertoire and Schumann's A minor will reconquer the place which, for the time being, it seems to have lost.

CHAPTER 4

CONTINUES THE FOREGOING BY
speculating on the recital's chances of survival in the
twenty-first century and touches upon the emergence in our
own times of the game of chance called 'Competition'

BUT I HAVE barely mentioned a more hopeful outlook and already I am
forced to admit that my last sentences are more in the nature of a pious
hope than a prophecy based on signs and portents. For these latter are the
opposite of hopeful. A recent article entitled 'The Vanishing Recital', after
tracing the gradual emergence of the present form of the recital and
describing the noticeable decline of this 'institution' (especially since 1955
or so), goes so far as to predict a return to the formula of the last third of
the nineteenth century of which the Milan programmes described a few
pages back give some idea. In the writer's words this would mean 'working
together in joint recitals or in groups, offering a variety of voices, of
instruments and of music'. Nor is this pessimistic voice an isolated one. In
1961 one of the most influential papers in the United States headlined an
editorial on this same subject: 'Vanished Glories of the Recitalist' and gave
as one of the reasons for the disaffection of the public the absence of
audience-compelling platform personalities of the Paderewski, Kreisler,
Rachmaninoff type. There are other reasons too.

It is symptomatic of the present status of the recital that a pianist of the
rank of Friedrich Gulda, who has made his name as an interpreter of Beethoven and the Viennese classics, nowadays captures audiences—mostly
young—with a hybrid form of concert, combining a first half of Bach,
Couperin and Ravel with a second half consisting entirely of jazz (some of it
of his own composition). His companions in this part of the programme
are a (jazz) double bass player and a percussionist of some repute, but he
also plays his own Prelude and Fugue in jazz style. In the large city on the

Continent where I saw this concert advertised his drawing power enables him to give it in the large hall, which as a rule only symphony concerts with prominent soloists can fill, recitals being usually given in the adjoining small hall. To make clear the 'split' character of the event, the most important daily of the city dispatched two reviewers to the concert, their music critic and their jazz expert, and the evaluations appeared fraternally side by side! This may well be—for the present, at any rate—an isolated case, but its success does strike one as a rather ominous symptom.

At a time when the numbers of the music-consuming public have grown immeasurably through the mass media, television and radio (television has invaded even the classroom and purports to offer master classes by illustrious instrumentalists), the selective listener inevitably withdraws from the concert hall into the privacy of his record listening room, where he can indulge his musical taste and sometimes, one may add, his fads.

The young artist, instead of gambling on début recitals in the music centres, nowadays prefers to play the 'game of chance' at some of the international contests which proliferate, and the knowledgeable minority therefore also withdraws from the concert hall. Those who used to be the 'kingmakers' in the concert hall and whose voice used to be heard at committee meetings of orchestras, chamber music societies and so on, can no longer exercise their self-appointed role of talent 'discoverers' and no longer go to these introductory recitals.

For good or ill, competitions are a major force in the world of music today. Bartók took a dim view of them; and he said, using the Hungarian word *verseny* which also means horse-racing; 'Competitions are for horses, not for musicians'. It is hardly necessary to point out that this gamble on the unforeseeable chances at competitions is incompatible with the slow maturing either of the performing personality or of the repertoire. Going from one competition to another, preparing the different *morceaux imposés*—Tchaikovsky or Paganini, Rachmaninoff or Chopin, Sibelius or Bartók, or Wieniawski—whether one has an affinity for the patron saints of these events or not, cannot be conducive to a development which only contact with the public, its resonance, its rejections, can bring about. On the contrary, a tendency to use gramophone recordings of the test pieces by illustrious interpreters as a crutch is an almost inevitable consequence of relying on competitions, with their mechanics of evaluation, instead of on

14

the '*vox populi*'. And these 'mechanics of evaluation' can be illustrated by a recent case history.

A competitor fails to reach the finals; I suggest that the voting be repeated; he does make the finals and is placed last, winning the equivalent of less than 200 dollars (a disappointing result for such good performances). Less than two months later, in another similar event, he is placed second against stiff competition and wins a prize of 2,000 dollars.

Instead of multiplying case histories of this sort, let us take a statistical look at the structure of these competitions and draw conclusions.

Competition A, to name no names, has only one prize. Twenty-three players apply, with *curriculum vitae,* etc., from whom, on the basis of their credentials, eleven are selected to play; three of these are chosen for the finals from which one winner emerges.

Competition B offers seven prizes. Some two dozen enter, all are heard by the jury and all but the seven prize-winners are eliminated. This is in order, as the saying goes, but if we look closer, we see that one of those who was eliminated had won the single, prestige-giving prize at Competition A two or three years before (this, I might add, puzzled some members of the jury at Competition B, as his performance there allowed us to infer neither past excellence nor promise for the future). Another of the eliminated candidates had won a prize at the previous year's Competition B, a shattering disappointment to the young artist who had—in my opinion—made progress in the intervening year. (The level of accomplishment was higher this time because of the participation of the superbly prepared and conditioned Soviet team who carried off the first three of the seven prizes.)

Competition C offers three prizes. There were thirty-seven entries of whom only eight reached the semi-finals. Here the amount of time spent by the jury in sorting out the wheat from the chaff is patently disproportionate to the project as a whole.

At Competition D all nineteen competitors were heard by both jury and public, and six won prizes. (A curious fact: the winner of the second prize at this marathon was placed, a few months later, fourth at Competition B.)

I should add—in order not to be misunderstood—that in all the competitions at which I have acted as member of the jury the voting showed satisfactory agreement among them and very little, if any, bias. A second round of voting was sometimes proposed in contested cases and minor adjustments resulted from this. Thus I am not questioning the actual procedure or the results, or the justice of the individual votes.

What is at the back of my mind is this: who is responsible for the decision of the majority of these young people (in some of the competitions the age limit is the grotesque one of thirty-five) to enter these competitions? It cannot be assumed that all of them suffer from delusions and act in a headstrong way without taking advice from their former teachers or those with whom they coach in the 'post-graduate' years. Once again I see myself nearing the conclusion (however hard I try to reject it) that some teachers condone the futile attempts of misguided pupils instead of discouraging them in time.

How often have we asked ourselves (and sometimes the fellow-juror sitting next to us) when a hopeless case in his or her late twenties was playing: how was it possible that none of the four or five teachers through whose hands they had passed in the course of fifteen or sixteen years of study had had the honesty to tell them the truth and nothing but the truth? Can it be that the private teachers whose livelihood happens to depend on giving lessons cannot 'afford', in every sense of the word, to tell the truth and lose a pupil? How can such teachers let these hopeless cases face competition after competition, always with the same result, the same frustration, the same hoping against hope for 'next time'?

It has become a cliché that we meet the same faces at these competitions, sometimes years and hundreds of miles apart. And it is poignant for a juror who happens to have a compassionate strain in him to read in the note before him that, since the last time, a new teacher has taken over. . . .

Out of these competitions a new type of semi-professional has grown up, neither fish nor flesh, not content with the pleasures of playing chamber music with friends, like his counterparts of forty or fifty years ago, but seeking a professional label. Aimless young men, young women with private means, having graduated from some conservatory with a diploma or scholarship, they take private lessons and, encouraged by their teachers, go from one competition to another, preparing *morceaux imposés* beyond their technical means. If they are lucky enough to gain a fourth or fifth prize, or an eleventh or twelfth—as they may, since all too often every one of a large number of prizes is awarded, however low the level of performance—they can call themselves 'lauréat du concours X' or 'a prize winner of the 19— competition at X', or, stretching the truth in a more

16

scandalous manner, '*the* prize winner of the 19— International Competition at X'. Even if they fail ever to reach the finals there are competitions which award a 'Diploma of Participation'. Any violinist who has served on a jury and seen, as I have, what pitiful figures these consolation prize winners cut in the competitions will be worried by this habit of misleading self-advertisement. We have no 'Food and Drug Act' to warn the consumer. Ineffectual teachers can go from one teaching appointment to another, distorting performances can be given on false authority, engagements made under false pretences.

Another pessimistic thought occurs: many of these misguided competitors own valuable instruments; is it perhaps not the teachers only but also the violin dealers who encourage them to pursue chimaeras?

I am not unconscious of the beneficial side effects which competitions can sometimes have on the opening phase of the career of deserving winners or of the occasional moments of elation which they provide for the, sometimes, sorely tried jurors. To discover an outstanding talent who has been well-taught, and to discover him some three years before he wins a major award, is a heady pleasure indeed. This was my experience when I first heard Konstantyn Kulka, a Polish boy then about fifteen years old, at the Genoa competition where I fought for his admission into the finals, was outvoted and—three years later saw him carry off the first prize in the Munich competition of 1966! But these are—alas—rare happenings, and the law of diminishing returns is beginning to make itself felt. As one impresario has put it: 'what is needed now is a competition among all the first prize winners of recent years. . . .'*

* *By the time these pages appear in print, three or more new competitions will have taken place: in Vancouver, B.C., London (Emily Anderson Award), Naples (Fondazione Alberto Curci) and probably others which have not come to my notice.*

CHAPTER 5

GLANCES AT THE INTERACTION OF
*competitions with the gramophone industry and contrasts
the slow maturing of the virtuosi of former generations (in
orchestral and teaching posts) with the mushroom-growth of
careers in our times*

IT IS NOT surprising that many performances by younger performers lack the stamp of authenticity, the mark of a personal view evolved through trial and error. I recently read this indictment after a reputedly most successful début: 'The performance suggested an exact photograph rather than the actuality.'

In the domain of gramophone recordings too, the young artist has to face new hazards, new in comparison to the recent past, when only that which the artist had made 'his own' in countless performances in the concert hall, used to be recorded. The 'artist and repertoire' men today, who like to feel themselves in the role of Svengali, can sway the newcomer to record immature 'Goldberg' Variations, all six of Schubert's violin–piano works, a dozen or so Mozart Violin Sonatas, complete Scriabin or Scarlatti Piano sets, and to take in their stride 'routine' matters like the six Bach Solo Sonatas. It was in 1919 that I first played the ten Beethoven Sonatas in a series and it was not until 1944 that they were recorded. Casals recorded the Six Cello Suites of Bach at the pace of two a year in the 1930s. With tape splicing, piecing together, reverberating, equalizing, these challenges can of course be met up to a point, but the question is how this hot-house forcing will ultimately work out for the young performer himself. A young virtuoso who is offered the chance of recording say, six or eight contemporary violin sonatas (Ravel, Debussy, Enesco, Bartók, Ives and others) that the company needs will not have the self-criticism or the self-abnegation to ask the company to wait until these works have slowly matured in him. It's either now or not at all.

All this sounds rather ominous but in a book that aims at a survey 'in the round', however swift and necessarily incomplete this has to be, unpalatable facts cannot be ignored. The dependence of young artists on competitions and on recordings is without doubt a fact of life.

The teenage prize-winner of a competition who is given a contract there and then to record the contemporary work with which he won the prize under the baton of its composer (who happened to be a member of the jury) and gets from the recording company the sensation-promoting press and radio 'treatment', has certainly found a short cut which all his talented classmates will dream about and aim for. (I am here outlining—though somewhat camouflaging—a recent case-history.) It will be useless to preach to them about the advantages of slow maturing, about going—in Schnabel's phrase—'the way of most resistance'! They can point to statements like this one, made by a young and remarkably gifted all-round musician, who has had extraordinary success as a pianist both on the platform and as a recording 'star'. 'The future of music will be measured by the future of recording. In our generation, the process of recording has begun to free itself from the memory of the public listening experience that shaped its earlier years. It has come to assert its autonomy—to define its own identity. Technology has made new acoustic values, new performing values (and for that matter, composing values too) available. Concerts as they are now known will not outlive the twentieth century.' With such statements to back up their philosophy and their attitudes, coming from a successful artist under forty, violinists will naturally shrug away any suggestion that playing in a good orchestra under a distinguished and demanding taskmaster, or accepting a teaching post, when they are around the age of twenty-five, might be one of the ways of maturing and of reaching their goal.

Busoni taught at the Helsinki and Moscow Conservatoires and at the Boston Conservatoire between the ages of twenty-three and twenty-eight, Hubay headed the violin classes at the Brussels Conservatoire when he was twenty-three and several violinists like Adolf Busch, Georg Kulenkampff and Wolfgang Schneiderhan—who subsequently became prominent soloists—had played in orchestras in their early twenties without their careers as soloists having suffered from this interlude. In this they had followed the example of their illustrious elders Joseph Joachim and Leopold Auer, who had become concertmasters in their late teens. Pierre Fournier was a member of the Pasdeloup Orchestra in Paris, 1925, and Francescatti of the Colonne Orchestra in 1930. Ysaÿe, Thibaud, Capet had all been members of an orchestra in their youth. I sometimes regretted having refused offers from Franz Schalk of the Vienna State Opera and Music Academy and from other institutions when I looked back upon the early stages of my development after I had reached the supposedly ripe age of forty or so. Carl Flesch in his *Art of Violin Playing,* which touches upon this question, as upon most of the other dilemmas in the soloist's life, writes: '. . . to the solo player who remains faithful to his special branch, some time spent in the orchestra, although only as a temporary measure, offers an uncommonly valuable means of extending his musical horizon.'

Who knows whether this wouldn't have led to my taking up the baton in later years? As it was, however, I let the chance go by when I was offered the opportunity to conduct a regular symphony programme in Rome in the 1920s; lack of experience as concertmaster prevented me from taking the plunge and taking advantage of this 'windfall'. . . . This spontaneous offer came from the observant administrator of the Symphony Society, who saw, while I was rehearsing as soloist, that I took greater interest in the doings of the orchestra than some soloists are wont to do and that my involuntary gestures proved my inner participation in what the orchestra was doing during the *tuttis,* too. Anyhow, this was the explanation given for his suggestion.

CHAPTER 6

AN OVER-AMBITIOUS ATTEMPT TO
compress into far too few pages alarming data about the
paucity of string players for orchestras in England, the
United States, Germany and France

I HAVE mentioned orchestral playing; and this brings us to a problem that is much discussed in our time and must be touched upon—however super-ficially—in any survey of the violin today: the dearth of orchestral violinists of a calibre compatible with the present high standard of performance. I do so against my better judgment, for to broach this controversial subject without being fully armed with statistics about the past, and about con-ditions up to the time of writing, is to court disaster. But all facets of our subject, violin teaching, the vicissitudes of the trained violinist's career, the influence on this career of the public, the gramophone industry, the mass media, the orchestral situation, the teaching profession, are so closely interwoven that I have to take the risk.

This question of finding adequate replacements in practically all orches-tras, everywhere, bristles with bewildering contradictions. Japanese orchestras advertise in the official German Orchestra Union Magazine, trying to fill the post of leader, but German orchestras entrust first desk positions to Japanese string players (known to be excellent, dependable orchestra men); English orchestras speak about a shortage of string players of sufficiently high standard, whereupon the Principal of one of the most respected educational institutions in London maintains that 'London is full' of efficient players, trained in these institutions. Yet one of London's finest orchestras was 'surprised' at the small number of applicants for the post of leader (in 1965), and in 1966 at one time in the three good orchestras in the provinces the leader's chair was 'in search of' its incumbent.

Germany used to 'export' its surplus of fine orchestral players to America in the not so remote past; now it answers advertisements like this one: 'American violinist, graduate of Oberlin College, speaks German.' In May 1965, only 36·4 per cent of the vacancies for violinists in German orchestras could be filled. In the same year one of the best opera orchestras in the country had only sixteen applicants for a first violin vacancy, as against about sixty between the wars. Some of the applicants were aged forty-three and only four of these had the background of a distinguished orchestra.

The audition procedure for this orchestra is: each applicant plays his solo (concerto), the three or six who are seriously considered are given excerpts from *Figaro, Così Fan Tutte, Magic Flute, Fidelio, Walküre, Siegfried, Rosenkavalier, Arabella, Falstaff*. A notoriously difficult slow, and one fast, excerpt from Siegfried is always demanded and a *sautillé* passage from the third act of *Così Fan Tutte*. It has sometimes happened, so my informant tells me, that the audition has no result and the vacancy remains unfilled. Women violinists have to be considerably better than men in order to be engaged. (In recent years three excellent women have been chosen.) It seems that what the younger applicants commonly lack is 'intellectual capacity and good *spiccato*'—whatever my informant means by grouping together these rather dissimilar attributes.

The official German orchestra magazine *Das Orchester* (February 1966) quotes a well-known conductor on his experiences with auditions: 'It is quite common to find that an applicant can play the Beethoven Concerto after a fashion (*schlecht und recht*), but fails when faced with a difficult passage in *Rosenkavalier*. Wouldn't it be better if the contrary were the case?'

A former concertmaster, now orchestral personnel manager of one of the world's most important opera houses, writes to me: 'One of our violinists recently proved his mettle as a recitalist in X Hall. In our orchestra he is completely worthless, gets lost, can't follow changes of tempo in spite of having been with us for four years. *La Bohème* is a pitfall for him.'

The papers read at the Tanglewood (U.S.A.) String Symposia, 1963 and 1964, were published by the Boston Symphony Orchestra under the Title 'String Problems—Players and Paucity'; the memorandum of the *Deutsche Orchestervereinigung* (1962) is entitled 'Diminishing Prestige of German Music Culture' and is a 148-page-long warning cry. It goes into all questions with true German thoroughness; discusses the rise in the standard of orchestral performance (caused partly by the recordings on disc, or on tape for broadcasts, with which the public can compare the live performances in their own home town; and also by the demands of contemporary scores); points out the discrepancy between the meagre material rewards of an orchestral player's career and his long years of study; and compares the Soviet state-sponsored music education, the incentives which the United States offers to students and to those entering the career, with the discouraging conditions in Germany and the resulting threat to the normal sources of replacement. (In 1953 those studying the violin in German music high schools and conservatoires were 38 per cent of the total enrolment, this percentage dropping in 1960 to 26 per cent.)

It is a curious phenomenon that in comparison with the violin situation there seems to be an abundance of good cellists. In a survey of the talent available both for the concert platform and for orchestras it would probably be difficult to match a list of the cellists with a list of violinists of the same stature, attainment or promise. The fact that at the 1966 Tchaikovsky Competition in Moscow cello entries were far more numerous than violin is unprecedented, and seems to bear out my surmise. Some thirty years ago, in the Feuermann-Piatigorsky-Cassadó era, the reverse would have been the case. (I am not mentioning the name of Casals, who, happily for us, is still a dominant factor in any discussion of cello playing, today, as sixty years ago.)

There are signs of awareness that this shortage of orchestral violinists needs fundamental treatment, that is, at an early stage of training. One of the best orchestra leaders in Germany has recently left his post to become head of the classes for orchestral training (*Orchesterübungen*); and Holland announces an 'International Violin Week' under a well-known orchestra leader who—presumably—will *not* follow the pattern of 'master classes' but will aim at improving the level of orchestral violinists.

A project known as Collegium Musicum has been started in Germany by Count Schonborn in his castle Pommersfelden in Lower Franconia, where a 100-piece orchestra of young players is given several weeks of symphonic training under an experienced conductor. No instrumental tuition, no so-called 'master classes', but the accent on ensemble, on group consciousness, on the faculty of listening to the next desk too!

Eugène Ormandy, conductor of the Philadelphia Orchestra, in a recent interview, visualised a three-year-course of symphony orchestra practice sessions three times a week, under the best conductors, which would give the apprentice symphony player 'the basic repertory'; but he did not give a blueprint for the realization of this laudable aim.

In the United States the Ford Foundation has shown with its 85 million dollar gift in 1965—to be spread among some fifty major orchestras—that it is fully aware of the gravity of the situation and has stated its objectives in very explicit terms: 'To advance quality by enabling more musicians to devote their major energies to orchestral performance: to strengthen symphonic organizations and enlarge the audience for orchestral music by permitting the orchestras to increase their seasons; to attract talented young people to professional careers by raising the income and prestige of orchestra members.' It is this last sentence that seems to me most significant from the point of view of these present pages, which are naturally destined mainly for educators and for young people who are about to decide the road they intend to take.

The National Council on the Arts (U.S.A.) also made a grant of $400,000 in 1966 with approximately the same objectives in mind: 'to help meet the shortage of qualified instrumentalists' and emphasizing the need for outstanding string players.

Although I do so with reluctance, I feel I owe it to my readers to reproduce the following pessimistic passages from a recent letter. The writer is Librarian of a distinguished Music School in New York City, a musicologist and former quartet and orchestra player: 'The rumours about the shortage of string players in the U.S.A. are true. We fear that in less than twenty years there will not be enough string players to replace the older generation, and symphony orchestras will go out of existence. The reason is that young musicians, after 8–12 years of study, find no steady employment, and not enough reward to base an existence or feed a family, with its rewards. Of course, the U.S. magazines, with characteristic Madison Avenue optimism and hypocrisy, speak about several hundred symphony orchestras. But only six or eight are 100 per cent professional, and less offer a yearly salary.

'The New York Philharmonic offers year-round employment only since last year. Most of the smaller orchestras have a season of from twelve to thirty-four weeks and even during the season the professionals—10 to 30 per cent of the orchestra—must work at the local radio station, restaurants, dance affairs or at a non-musical job. The high cost of living makes orchestras a deficit-proposition forever and smaller cities cannot raise the money. Meanwhile, the universities try to push their musical programmes in fierce competition. It is a bitter farce.'

Contradictions face me when I try to supplement these notes with some case histories.

The fifty-six-year-old concertmaster of one of the major orchestras in America with thirty-four years' orchestral experience quits a post he has held for twenty years. The reasons: he wishes to take a year off for travel in Europe, then settle in some American city with a 'relaxed' schedule. On the other hand the well-liked and esteemed concertmaster of one of America's top orchestras, nearing the retirement age of sixty-five, will take another similar assignment (in a city where—I presume—a more 'relaxed schedule' will be possible!) as soon as he has reached it. His successor, who has been chosen after more than forty violinists have been auditioned, is a forty-year-old, extremely gifted virtuoso, who has had virtually no symphony repertory experience but has 'worked' the free-lance 'commercial' circuit for most of his professional life.

Four string players of another great orchestra in America band together as a quartet, obtain an appointment at one of the universities and tender their resignation to the orchestra; but it refuses to release them from their contract, saying that they cannot be replaced within the next few months.

One wonders: over forty players audition for one post, and two violinists who want to branch out in a quartet are said to be impossible to replace.

The lists of entrants in competitions filled to overflowing, Summer Courses by men of fine reputations in England, the United States, Switzerland, Italy, Portugal, all have a big enrolment and still, when it comes to filling string vacancies, some orchestras have to resort to advertising in daily papers—something that never used to be necessary; announcements in Musicians' Union magazines and the grapevine used to be enough. (*The Times* of London recently carried an advertisement: 'XYZ Orchestra, Sub Principal Violin—Vacancy'.)

The 130-page report of the French Ministry of Cultural Affairs (1963) on the problems facing music generally came to the conclusion that the state should take one of the four Paris orchestras under its wing, give high subsidies to the three other orchestras and—in the interest of healthy decentralization—found two new orchestras in two cities in the provinces (with a minimum of sixty musicians each), two high-level chamber orchestras and underwrite two string quartets.

In England the Report to the Calouste Gulbenkian Foundation entitled

'Making Musicians' (1965) gave a very thorough survey of all these problems (although curiously enough it failed to mention the comparatively new factor that had entered the picture: competitions).

Regarding the shortage of fully trained players, especially in strings, the opinion of the managements of leading orchestras and their principal players is unanimous. Lack of familiarity with the repertoire, insufficiently high standard of sight-reading ability, reluctance to submit to discipline, are mentioned in this report.

Among the reasons given for this state of things, there is one which seems to me particularly worthy of attention: the disappearance of theatre, spa and municipal orchestras in which young players on leaving college could earn a living while equipping themselves by experience for the higher standards of the first-rate orchestras.

CHAPTER 7

SPECULATES ON THE REASONS FOR THIS
state of things, questions whether the tuition right from the
early stages onwards is at fault and, in addition, offers some
case histories that may help to explain generalities (just
as statistical data may help to clarify case-histories)

THESE ARE unrelated facts only, cited at random, and unless we try to correlate them with the other symptoms that have been touched upon in the preceding pages, they will not lead us to a diagnosis of the causes. At this point I ask myself: isn't the absence of a sense of direction in the early teaching at the root of it all? Isn't it the competitive spirit among teachers, who are eager to 'show results', which in turn conditions their pupils to the sporting and gambling elements of the international competitions and prevents them from devoting sufficient time to *ensemble* playing, to sight-reading and generally to a broadening of their musical horizon? Heinrich Neuhaus, the teacher of Horowitz, Richter and Gilels, considers that the daily playing through of symphonies in four-hand arrangements, sight-reading, commerce with the inexhaustible treasure store of chamber music, should take up a major portion of the young *virtuoso*'s practice time. This is something that harks back to more leisurely, nineteenth-century days. Perhaps it is all the more necessary in our days when the *virtuoso* career has acquired a competitive angle that is far from wholesome.

Horowitz, whom I saw during holiday time in Switzerland in the early 1930s, at the beginning of his meteoric career, remained true to these principles of Neuhaus. He was at the time engrossed in the Beethoven Symphonies, in Liszt's transcription, playing Beethoven Sonatas with me, without any thought of ulterior 'utility'. Cortot, when he had won first prize at the Paris Conservatoire, announced to his parents (who had made sacrifices to enable him to finish his studies), 'Now I can begin to study in earnest', and he went to Bayreuth in the modest role of a *'corrépétiteur'*. I get glimpses of this spirit from some of my Japanese pupils. One who came to me after having won first prize at the Paris Conservatoire and various prizes at the Genoa (Paganini) and Geneva competitions, copies out in a calligraphic hand the text of the Preface to the third volume of the Joachim –Moser *Traité*, which I lend him, buys pocket scores of Bartók Quartets, which he hasn't yet played, and acquires also a plaster bust of Beethoven, out of his meagre allowance from home (his father is a violin teacher), to 'decorate' his modest room in the gardener's cottage near my house. He has more of 'Jean Christophe' in his make-up than most of the European or American students that I have come across.

Another Japanese pupil, a girl, who studied for two or three years at the Leningrad Conservatoire, alternates concert tours in Japan and the United States with periods of study with me. She occasionally sends me tapes of her concert performances, which I then comment upon by letter. A resounding victory at one of the international competitions and the beginnings of an international career seem to have made no difference to her attitude. Every absence of a few months is followed by months of study in our village. . . .

The European and American opposite numbers of these dedicated young Japanese, on the contrary, pin their hopes on competitions and on so-called 'master classes' and 'summer courses' of a few weeks' duration in different countries and under various teachers, who, by the nature of things, can do no more than point out generalities and are forced to ignore basic problems: they are what could be called guest teachers of guest pupils!

Of course, the results of such two or three-week 'workshops' depend to a great extent on the devotion and pedagogic flair of the master teacher and also on the attitude of the young people who sit at his feet. I hear that the recent initiative of one of the orchestras in Holland who joined forces with the conservatoire of that city in bringing over from America an out-standing cellist for a two-week course, had excellent results! But in some of these summer courses and master classes—and in their *reductio ad absurdum,* the one-afternoon 'master-class' given by world-famous figures to gatherings of 300 or more—the photographer's camera and the television producer play too preponderant a role, so it seems to me. As a distinguished colleague, both brilliant *virtuoso* and dedicated teacher, recently put it, it is not master classes that are needed, but 'real teaching, technique and repertory'. And he added: 'The phrase, "master class" has a double implication—it means that there is not only a master teacher but future master players as students, and that is too often not the case.' Here let me interpolate a typical case history: American, born 1942, studied with father and probably other teachers as well; 1962: one year with an illustrious *virtuoso*; 1963: with a fine *virtuoso* who also teaches; 1964: graduated from a big European conservatoire, private lessons with four other teachers.

One of the explanations for the dearth of string players for symphony orchestras that occurs to me is that our young players of this easy-going type avoid the commitment that an engagement for a few seasons in a symphony orchestra inevitably means. Advancement from one of the last desks to the first or second one has to be earned, earned by dedication to one's work, by the capacity to integrate oneself into an organism with a definite character of its own, something that every orchestra of standing has. The conductor of such an orchestra is quick to spot any unusual vigilance and enthusiastic co-operation on the part of a new and young member and seldom fails to recompense it with advancement. But then this is the hard way.

The dozens of chamber orchestras with their sometimes short seasons and fluctuating memberships (I have known cases where the new member joins the group twenty hours before the first concert), seem more attractive to this type of young player. And this in spite of the sometimes ludicrously inadequate pay (which the majority of these semi-professionals or downright amateurs accept, but which professionals with self-respect should by rights reject). He need not commit himself for any length of time, the repertoire does not offer the challenges that a symphony season does, the prospect of sightseeing on tours is alluring and so is the feeling of remaining available in case—to quote Mr Micawber—'anything should turn up'. This seems to me one of the main reasons for this much publicized paucity of qualified symphony players.

I don't think there have ever been a greater number of analytical publications dealing with string problems than now, nor as many summer courses everywhere. This, and the number of entries for the competitions, seems to disprove the theory that the number of string players is dwindling. The Moscow and the Montreal competitions took place at the same time in June 1966, and each attracted over thirty-five competitors for the ten prizes each had to offer; and the severe repertoire requirements of course automatically eliminated hundreds of would-be contestants. . . . When one considers this, the available reservoir of violinists does not seem so small. Rather it is that these students, buyers of didactic books, members of short-lived chamber *ensembles* and all these contestants in competitions set their sights to other careers than that of a symphony orchestra player.

These interludes with chamber orchestras (since they are all playing worthwhile music) do not bar the young string player from other commitments later on: in a teaching post, in a full-time symphony orchestra or in a string quartet. But a certain twenty-six-year-old American who came to consult me recently found out that there is such a thing as a 'point of no return'. After studying with a local man, then for two years with a teacher of international reputation and for another year with a respected old chamber musician, he thought he could with impunity go into 'commercial' playing, and it so happened that he became a 'captive' there for four years. Now after these barren four years during which he toured incessantly with a band of four violinists, four saxophones, three trumpets, three trombones, double basses and percussion, playing the dreariest kind of night-club and dance-hall music, he came to me in his *désarroi* and I had the sad duty of explaining to him what havoc these last years had wrought with his playing, which must have been quite promising when he was in his teens. The courage with which he reacted to my rather shattering diagnosis and the considerable composing skill which he had acquired in his teens hold out some hope that he may yet be able to make a fresh start. But how different his path would have been had he joined a fine symphony orchestra in his late teens and withstood the financial lure of 'commercial' music. But young players seem no longer to be sufficiently attuned to the idea of a few years' apprenticeship under a demanding taskmaster. They prefer to gamble on competitions, short chamber orchestra engagements, commercial music, taping out-of-the-way repertoire for the broadcasting systems in the vain hope that they will some day be 'discovered' in this way. Anything rather than a few years in an orchestra.

A music-loving artist with pen and brush, Alfred Bendiner, in his album of caricatures of famous musicians (mainly those who appeared with the great orchestra of his home town, Philadelphia), entitled *Music To My Eyes*, writes: 'I doubt if anybody in the audience can sit through a whole concert and listen to every note and enjoy it thoroughly. The people who enjoy a concert are the members of the orchestra themselves. If you are ever fortunate enough to go backstage when the orchestra comes off, you will find them all in good humour.' Can it be that the joy has gone out of this 'communal activity which poses most of the problems of the world at large'—as one of our outstanding younger conductors has called it?

He goes on to say: 'we need to work for something bigger than ourselves, even though we fight so hard to assert our individuality.' It is this 'something bigger than ourselves' that makes for the elation that I have so often witnessed backstage, when the orchestra comes off the platform and when some of the principal players crowd around the conductor discussing fine points in the performance, the glow of which is still upon them.

A former orchestral player in a recent article disagrees with the generally voiced opinion that there is a serious string shortage, but thinks that it is rather the absence of this glow, this elation, that makes qualified players turn their backs on an orchestral career. Writing probably from personal experience he says that the player 'is beaten down by sarcastic remarks, very often personal, and his love for music flies out of the window. The conductors are primarily responsible for this condition . . . these musical dictators who are complaining about the lack of talent, themselves are to blame. I know of two former students at the Curtis Institute who are now medical doctors.'

And he concludes by putting his hope in the Ford Foundation plan which is to improve matters and ensure 'better salaries, better conductors(!) and better travelling conditions. . . .'

To show these contradictory evaluations in a still more glaring light let me put down here a recent case history: a new 'chamber symphony' orchestra of thirty-six musicians was formed: 1,042 musicians applied (during one year) for these thirty-six posts, and 394 were given auditions! Even if we deduct from these auditions those that were given to wind players, the number of string auditions must still have been staggering. (By the way: the concertmaster chosen for this chamber symphony orchestra is a recent winner of the first prize at the Genoa Paganini Competition.) One should remember at this point that there were only eighteen applicants for the vacant first violin chair in one of the important opera orchestras in Germany, mentioned some pages back.

Equally staggering must have been the ignorance about facts of life of the majority of those who submitted to these auditions. They apparently neither realized how much nowadays is demanded of a player in an ensemble of high rank, nor were they able to evaluate their own capacities (or rather incapacity) and visualize themselves in such a group. (It is the same kind of blissful ignorance that we members of juries at international competitions encounter time and again in the first 'rounds'.)

As we have seen, the French Ministry of Cultural Affairs believes one of the remedies for the present unsatisfactory situation is establishment of two more orchestras. There is also talk of creating an orchestra of first-prize winners of the Paris Conservatoire, there being so many of these 'premiers prix'. . . .

London, on the other hand, has twice as many orchestras now as it had thirty years ago and string vacancies are increasingly difficult to fill. The recent resignation at the age of below forty of one of the best concert-masters I know, from one of the most important posts, indicates another facet of the present situation.

Carl Flesch, in a passage I shall quote in the next chapter, refers to a 'certain psychic bondage' to the conductor. This might be the clue to several resignations from concertmasters' posts which seem surprising to the outsider. The artist suddenly feels stifled, and wants to exchange the security of his position for the adventure to be found in freedom of expression, in the soloist's or chamber musician's life, in spite of all its uncertainties.

Resentment of the same 'psychic bondage' may also explain why it is so difficult to fill the post of assistant, or deputy, concertmaster, and that of second violinist in a fine string quartet. Not only the conductor but a masterful concertmaster, or first violin of a string quartet, can bring out latent inferiority complexes and frustrations in these 'second-in-commands'. As a second violinist in a quartet recently put it: 'If a violinist is good enough for the job, he's going to want to leave it.' Leave it he did, and to bolster up his morale—I surmise!—gave a solo recital before starting to build a new quartet with himself as first violin. . . .

Here I am, gathering such facts and information as come to me, and none the wiser as to the basic question: is it a matter of too few string players for too many orchestras?

Or is it rather that there are too few orchestras for too many string players?

CHAPTER 8

BEGINS WITH A DICTUM OF CARL FLESCH
about the importance of the orchestral player in the state of
music in general and about the sins of omission and commission
of teachers, which in turn leads into saddening data concerning quacks,
spurious claims and the like

At this point let me draw the reader's attention to the summing-up of the orchestra string players' many problems and many questionings which he can find in Carl Flesch's *Art of Violin Playing* (pp. 77–80). Although published in 1923 (and therefore—we may assume—probably written almost fifty years ago) these pages contain so much that is still pertinent to the changed conditions of the day that a few of these statements should be given here, out of context.

First of all: Flesch does not hesitate to call the orchestra violinist 'that member of the musical confraternity who is most important to the cultivation of music in general'. He goes on to say: 'Exactly as in the state where the middle classes, together with the farmer who tills the soil, represent the most valuable, because the most permanent kernel of the entire body social around which the upper and lower circles crystallize, so the plane on which the orchestra musician and, in particular, the orchestra violinist stands, above all determines the general level of the musical-reproductive art of any land. The general contemporary level of violin playing depends only secondarily on the quality and quantity of the soloist.' Speaking of the composer's dependence on the capacity of the orchestra to realize his imaginings (so often ahead of their time!) he writes: 'This reciprocal influence of creator and orchestra musician is determinant for the development of musical art as a whole.'

With all this Flesch does not gloss over the 'tragedy of the orchestra violinist's career', which he describes in some detail and finds that these tragedies, this 'mental embitterment' due to 'a certain psychic bondage' (Flesch is speaking about the inner resistance of player to conductor) must be blamed to a certain extent on the teacher's misguidance, 'misrepresentation of fact', particularly in the early stages of tuition. And he ends these pages by admonishing the teaching profession not only to aim at developing proficient orchestra players but to remember that 'the education of an efficient tribe of concertmasters is one of the most important tasks devolving upon the profession.'

Martin Marsick used to tell his pupil Jacques Thibaud, in whom he foresaw the great soloist he was to become: 'You'll have to follow the ranks, you might have to put up with one of the last desks in a symphony orchestra or even in a theatre or café ensemble. This mustn't discourage you: it'll help towards developing your talent and what is also important: your character.'

While writing these pages I am constantly made aware of the sins of omission on the part of the teaching profession that Carl Flesch was admonishing almost half a century ago.

It is the laudable exceptions who show up those members of the profession who fail to make their pupils conscious of the facts of life, and allow them to live in a fool's paradise from one fruitless competition to the next. One conscientious teacher put the question in a letter to me in these sentences: 'What is one's moral obligation if a pupil wants to enter a competition one knows very well he does not stand any chance of winning? I have just refused to endorse the application of a pupil of mine for the Moscow contest. . . .' Were the majority of the teaching profession imbued with such moral scruples, the orchestral situation would be quite different.

This cursory glance at the problems surrounding our instrument, however superficial, still does not result in any sort of diagnosis or suggestion for improvement. My rhetorical question a few pages back, whether it isn't the absence of a sense of direction in the early stages of our teaching that is at fault, may already have indicated the line I am about to follow.

Let me preface this by admitting that strictly speaking, I am not qualified to go into these questions in any other capacity than as a sort of unofficial observer, an observer from the outside. I have not taught in a regular way for several decades now (my last teaching year at the Geneva Conservatoire was 1923–4), but these last few years have brought me in contact with

34

many 'finished' violinists ('finished' as the saying goes) who come to consult me at some critical phase of their career; also sitting on the jury at competitions in Brussels, London, Moscow, New York, Budapest, Paris, Genoa, and Munich, has given me so much insight into what goes on in conservatoires and in the private studios of well-known teachers that I can hazard some generalizations after all. One of these is that students seem more inclined than formerly to put their faith in different systems, methods, schools, changing from one to the other at the drop of a hat.

A 'get-rich-quick' attitude—translated into violinistic terms—causes pedagogues and publishers to cater to precisely these tendencies. Publishers advertise works that are (I am quoting from a blurb) 'a real product of the union of violin art and science', that 'outdistance in utility and as a means to rapid development all that has gone before—without exception'. They offer 'studies in tenths' (notoriously dangerous if practised in indiscriminate and excessive doses!), and promise that these will 'maintain technical equipment of both arms' and 'improve it to the utmost finesse'. Another publication will 'provide the means for the highest development of the power of the mind to discipline the physical equipment of the instrumentalist' and 'lead to the innervation of the mental, the nervous and the muscular factors'. A 'perpetual motion' in fingered octaves is offered to the student who, if he succumbs to this sporting prowess challenge and practises it in indiscriminate doses (as youngsters are likely to do) may reap a more or less serious muscle injury from such excesses. (Carl Flesch repeatedly sounds a warning note about this while his brother, Dr Julius Flesch, in his book, *Berufs-Krankheiten des Musikers* (Niels Kampmann Verlag, 1925), describes several pathological case histories from his medical practice.) As in several similar cases it is obvious that the fingerings are based on abstract imaginings, pen in hand, and are not really 'laboratory tested'. Other exercises, practised fifteen minutes a day, guarantee 'a solid foundation for a brilliant and infallible left-hand technique', and it is promised that they will 'open new fields for dazzling technical feats'. Courses are offered to 'Advanced and Artist Violinists, who are frustrated' in a 'new MIRACULOUS concept of holding the bow'—('10 lessons by app. 500 dollars'). They no longer need 'despair because of loss of control and stiffening of both right and left arms and fingers'. 'There is nowhere', declares the latest advertisement that has come to my notice, 'in the voluminous literature of violin playing any material dedicated to the smooth transition of the melody from string to string.' Hence the necessity for yet another work 'commended' by a string of eminent masters. These are extreme cases, of course, and are not typical of the claims that the majority of teachers and publishers of pedagogical works make. (And, anyway, we meet this type of advertising in other domains as well.) I only bring this up because of its significance as a symptom. Such *offers* would not come into the open if the latent *demand* did not make itself felt.

It is no consolation to find that these discoverers of 'secrets' (Paganini's and other violinists') emerge from time to time and are not entirely a symptom of our days.

A book, published in 1927 in Paris, prescribes exercises for the strengthening of the violinist's muscles that are supposed to bring him in twenty minutes results that only four or five hours of 'work with the instrument' could obtain for him. A chair, to be lifted shoulder high, a contraption called '*musculeur*', the steel coils of which have to be stretched by two handles, a so-called 'extender' (which the violinist has to activate while he 'performs' the movement of change of position), exercises with 'sandow' apparatus, playing while leaning on the left leg and hip and swinging the right leg in all directions, these are only a few of the 'aids' for left-hand technique.

For the bow arm a separate set of instruments has to be used: an 'extensor' which has to be opened and shut while the wrist is moving back and forth, simulating a '*détaché*' bowing; a wooden roll, approximately the size of a roll of paper kitchen towels, on which a canvas band, weighted by an iron dumb-bell, is suspended. The violinist holds the wooden roll at shoulder height and in rolling it, pulls the weighted canvas band up, by the action of the rolling movement of the fingers and thumb of his right hand. This procedure is supposed to be—I quote—'excellent for strengthening the thumb, index finger, fifth finger and wrist in addition to all the muscles useful in bowing.' The iron dumb-bell can also be used for the following exercise: hold it at the right knob and turn it clockwise and counter-clockwise. The author recommends the use of larger and heavier dumb-bells in proportion to the 'development the muscles undergo' through these exercises. . . . And this happened in 1927.

Students nowadays flit from one teacher to another, from one violin 'centre' to another, hoping for salvation from a massive dose of Bach one summer, an immersion in chamber music during another summer holiday, a visit to Paris with the avowed intention of acquiring '*legèreté*' (I am quoting faithfully from what one young German violinist told me after a competition at which he did not reach the finals)—all this is symptomatic of a certain inner restlessness, insecurity, dissatisfaction.

A guitarist wrote quite recently to suggest my joining forces with him: 'Paganini was a guitarist and I think it would be a fine idea to teach a class of violinists how to play the guitar.'

It seems to me that a book like mine, which hopes to avoid the pitfalls of yet another 'how to' manual, is the place to speak about such symptoms and about the '*Zeitgeist*' that brings them forth.

CHAPTER 9

MAINLY ABOUT A DIDACTIC PUBLICATION
that—on the contrary—makes no such claims but proceeds
serenely on its honest, musically health-giving course

THE PUBLICATIONS, summer classes, courses of initiation into hitherto 'unknown' techniques and procedures mentioned in my previous chapter all appear to pay their way. But in comparison with these, the Bartók forty-four Violin Duets, which will be the subject of the last chapter but one of this book, and the *Doflein Method*, to which they are related ideologically as part of the same educational scheme,* deserve infinitely wider diffusion all over the world than they have yet received.

Both works were published in the early '30s. The five volumes of the *Doflein Method* have attained a circulation of about 250,000; but this does not seem to me commensurate with its worth. It can, I think, be called a pilot effort in that it builds up the musical and violinistic foundation by strictly musical means, right from the beginner stage. Bartók, Carl Orff, Hindemith, Matyas Seiber, H. Genzmer, P. Kadosa and others contributed to it, and in some cases wrote 'made to measure' pieces (mostly violin duets) for it: and there are judiciously chosen Etudes by Leopold Mozart, Montclair, Campagnoli, Kayser, Spohr, Alard, Beriot and excerpts from works that command respect in every case. Technical problems are not neglected or glossed over; to prepare the student for intelligently phrased playing of these pieces they alternate with short but 'to the point' technical exercises. And among the examples in the later volumes are musical equivalents of tongue-twisters which will serve both as sight-reading tests and as practice for the future orchestral violinist.

But what I find most unexpected and welcome are the short exercises (always musically attractive and always for two violins, that is, for the

* See article by E. Doflein in 'Revue Musicale', Bartók issue, No. 224, Paris 1955.

38

teacher-pupil team) written by Erich Doflein and aimed, not at virtuosity, but at style; such, for instance, as: 'change of position on a repeated note, involving a change of strings' or 'direct entry into the fourth or fifth position' or a note like this (for the Trio of Haydn's Quartet No. 38): 'The fingering is the composer's; the reason for including this excerpt being that in it Haydn's intention that the first violinist should slide upward in the Haydnesque manner on slurred intervals of thirds or fourths, or downward on sevenths (with 4–2 or 4–1) is made explicit (and is authenticated).' There are also whole-tone scale exercises, 'diminished fourths between first and fourth fingers', 'minor sixths', etc., figurations that prepare the pupil for some of the demands of contemporary music.

Thus the difficulty of the sequences in minor sixths in Bartók's Second Concerto (for instance, at No. 284, First Movement) will have been anticipated to some extent by the exercises in minor sixths in the fifth volume of the *Doflein Method*.

The very fact that the author makes teacher and pupil conscious of the necessity of 'raising the bow slightly between slurred notes' (the title of a sub-section with examples by Mozart, J. Playford (1652), eighteenth-century composers, Bartók and a nineteenth-century pedagogue of proven merit like H. E. Kayser) shows that we are here in the presence of a musician-violinist and not of a compiler obsessed by means while losing sight of ends.

He is guiding teachers and pupils in a direction that will counterbalance the often one-sided cultivation of the left hand: speed, intonation, ever-present *vibrato* and so on, by directing attention to the bow-arm and to the enormous importance it has in determining the 'style' of a performance, the musical sense, the intelligibility, the convincing quality of a phrase or of a page or of a whole movement. When it comes to bowing, there are many things in our equipment that we take for granted because the talented few inevitably find a solution for these problems through trial and error. However, violin methods being designed not for the 'talented few' but for the great bulk of those whose sights are set for more modest objectives in our musical life, it is necessary that problems should be given a name and their solution presented to the pupil intelligibly. Thus it is refreshing to find a chapter sub-heading entitled 'Manipulation of the bow for strokes of unequal duration' (the user of the English edition of the Doflein will have

Ds

to condone the sometimes clumsy, too literal translations from the German!). He will also find that the *Siciliano* rhythm ♪·♫ , the *Gigue* bowing

 (so important in much eighteenth-century music), the syncopated

bowings, *spiccato* with string crossing, 'mixed bowings' ♪♫ and so on are given the attention they merit and that thus it will not be the unhappy lot of the conductor to have to explain and demonstrate these bowings to similarly unhappy second violinists at the third or fourth desk while rehearsing Beethoven's Seventh! . . .

To clarify my thoughts further: it is *before* tackling a 'simple' phrase like this one in Mozart's Concerto in D (K. 218), First Movement:

Ex. *1*

that the student has to be made conscious of the role of the bow in giving each segment of four notes on the three different strings their individuality by a subtle phrase separation (it would be too much to say, 'raising the bow slightly!') while preserving the unity and meaningfulness of the phrase as a whole. (The role of fingering in achieving this 'variety in unity' is self-evident, but without the intervention of a bow-arm trained in such subtleties, it would not be sufficient in itself.) Play it in the first position with unarticulated, 'flat' bow-strokes of a uniform 'thickness', and you will see what Leopold Mozart meant when he wrote that sentence about the 'two notes slurred under one bow' in his *Violin School*!

It is only my fear of seeming to write a 'blurb' for this work that makes me stop. Educational efforts of this type do need a shot in the arm. The lack of curiosity of teachers is such that a worthwhile and musically delightful little volume (this one also of the 1930s) destined for beginners, the *Geigenbüchlein* by the Vienna composer Hugo Kauder (Universal Edition), has been allowed to go out of print. These short pieces by a composer who in a secondary activity happens to be also a violin pedagogue belong to that rare species, music that is deceptively simple, pursues very definite aims, technically speaking, while giving the beginner insight into musical form, diction, phrasing, metrical sophistication, in a way that the accredited 'Violin Methods' and 'Violin Tutors' of the turn of the century seldom do. To these 'casualties' of the music-publishing trade belong also Benjamin Britten's and Antonio Brosa's compilation of violin passages, published by Boosey & Hawkes about two decades ago and now out of print.

All this seems to me symptomatic and should make us ponder.

CHAPTER 10

AN UNSUCCESSFUL ATTEMPT TO
sum up, and an admission that a computer could do this better

BEFORE CONCLUDING this somewhat pessimistic first part, in which I have aimed at a look 'in the round' at the complex world of violin-playing, let me give some opinions of others, which I believe will corroborate my own findings.

Remembering the dictum of Carl Flesch which I quoted at the beginning of Chapter 8, I have tried, in writing these pages, to bear in mind the numerically immense middle class of violinists, and here the opinion of George Szell, whose prowess not only as a great conductor but as an educator has become proverbial, carries great weight. The emergence of his Cleveland Orchestra as one of the three or four great orchestras in the world is the most eloquent testimony to his expertise in matters of string-playing. I leave out of account for the purposes of this book the mastery which gave the other sections of his orchestra their superb quality and enabled him to weld them into one instrument. What concerns us here are his opinions about the present state of string-playing, his experiences at auditions which, the Cleveland Orchestra being what it is, yield a cross-section of the best available talent.

His feeling—and this tallies with mine, as can be seen in many of the preceding pages—is that present-day violin tuition suffers from various musical and instrumental shortcomings and neglects. He says that musically the students very often lack even elementary theoretical knowledge, are poor sight-readers because they have not gone through serious *solfège* classes and have no conception of style.

Instrumentally the most striking common quality is the lack of development of the bow-arm. Everything in their tuition seems to have been

42

concentrated on producing as big a sound as possible and having as swift a left hand as possible. Any subtle function of wrist and fingers of the right hand is practically unknown to them. Therefore while they are able to go through some of the concerti, particularly the *cantabile* passages, with some semblance of brilliance, they are completely helpless when confronted with, say a second violin part of a Mozart symphony, with its problems.

They have never been told that the bow has to articulate the music. Very few of them know how to play near the frog. Many of them, because of the stiffness of wrist and fingers, have no smooth bow change on either end. Generally speaking, these students are trained and coached solely with a view to the soloist's career, which of course only a very small percentage of them can make anyway, whereas all preparation that would enable them to be relatively happy and not disgruntled members of orchestras or chamber ensembles is completely neglected.

They are not taught, or not sufficiently taught, chamber music and ensemble techniques and, moreover, they are not stimulated to love music as such, instead of loving only themselves and their careers.

To this letter Szell adds a postscript about 'those violin graduates knowing so damned little good music' and about the failure of teachers to use first violin parts of Beethoven Quartets as technical as well as musical teaching material. The director of chamber music at one of America's biggest music schools entirely concurs with George Szell's opinion.

We are more likely to find this 'loving music as such' among amateurs than in the ranks of professionals. One of my correspondents, Father X of the Carmelite order, writes to me about the 'satisfaction and joy' it must be to a 'real artist' to be 'expressing one's fine feelings by means of co-ordination between the mind and a violin and a bow and ten obedient fingers'.

In a recent article John Celentano states: 'Symphony orchestra conductors, personnel managers and others responsible for the maintenance of excellence in our symphonic organizations view with increasing concern the results of the periodic string auditions. The auditions reveal many excellent performers, some of virtuoso calibre, but few musicians. Generally, the solo material is well prepared while the reading lacks style and phrasing, even in the "experienced" player. It is easy to understand how a

43

good string performer can play his solo material well, and then read a Mozart symphony string part with a total lack of style and phrasing.

Unlike the reconstructive process of learning a concerto, where the musical significance of each note, each bar, each phrase, is slowly hammered out by finding the correct mechanical means and through a repetitive process committed to memory, the mechanical reaction in reading the Mozart string part demands instantaneous recognition of the musical function of the part at any given moment as it contributes to the musical unity of the entire score. At first glance the appearance of the material should reveal its style. Instinctively certain elements of that style will condition the manner of reading: use of the bow, phrasing, passage work, embellishments—even the quality of the tone. One of the best-known teachers in Europe whom I questioned about any 'misfits' that might have turned up at the Sibelius contest in Helsinki (1965) at which he acted as member of the jury wrote to me: 'Every jury-member could give any figure between 0 and 25 and when I compared the figures of myself to those of others, I was in some cases highly surprised. There were for instance cases when I gave 17 for a candidate and another jury member gave to the same player only 4! Thus to the particular jury-member this candidate must have appeared a misfit, while to me this was a very acceptable average player. To my mind, the standard of the whole was fairly good, though not first-class. The overall impression of violin playing as such was on a pretty high level, while questions of artistry, music-making, style, intelligence and interpretation were fairly poor. Most candidates played their Paganini-Caprices very well indeed, while their Bach and Mozart were very poor. While in my opinion the playing-standard varied considerably, it was on the whole more or less acceptable, though (as I mentioned before) in no case first-class; but as a misfit I could personally only think of one single case.'

I should find an attempt at a conclusive summing-up on the basis of the case histories, symptoms, data, contained in these few dozen pages somewhat presumptuous; it is, I think, more honest to admit defeat. All the contradictory evidence and data and statements that I have assembled do not help me to formulate a clear-cut policy, and come to constructive conclusions. Perhaps feeding these into a computer would give us the answer.

Part II

CHAPTER 11

EXAMINES THE QUESTION WHETHER
a change of string is more acceptable on a semitone than on a whole tone

THE FIRST subject I propose to discuss is one of those that may cause the reader to exclaim: 'But I knew this all along.... That goes without saying!' And still it needs to be discussed. Even if—like myself—the student has instinctively avoided something that has been handed down from the comfortable 'bad old days' he should nevertheless be made aware of it and avoid it consciously.

The 'something' in question is the jarring effect that *change of strings on a semitone* has *in legato passages* (and elsewhere too). The change on a whole tone interval is much less objectionable.

It is—as so often!—the 'comfortable' third position that causes us to put up with bumpy transitions from one string to another, like

Ex. 1

when we could so easily effect the change of string on a whole tone in the same context.

A few examples will make this clear: Beethoven, Op. 12, No. 1, second movement,

Ex. 2

any other fingering would be better than the routine one in the example above; by stretching the first finger back between D and C sharp and going into the second position (and later into the fourth position) we would effect the change smoothly. Starting in the second position and using occasionally the third position thus

Ex. 3

would be another solution.

Even playing it in the fourth position (but stretching back the first finger on the G sharps) would be more acceptable to sensitive ears than the time-honoured fingering (third position). In theory, playing it in the first position would also be possible, but the primitiveness of this fingering would go against the grain.

A few examples will show how often we are guilty of this thoughtlessness in changing strings on a semitone, when this could so easily be avoided. Changes on a semitone are marked with an asterisk. The lower fingerings are mine.

Bach Sonata II. Violin and
Clavier. Andante un poco
(3rd bar)

Vitali Chaconne

Ex. 4

Ex. 5

Bach Sonata III. Violin and Clavier. First movement. Adagio

Ex. 6

Beethoven Sonata Op. 30, No. 3. Third movement. Allegro vivace.

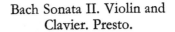

Ex. 7

Mozart Concerto K. 219. Adagio.

Ex. 8

Bach Sonata II. Violin and Clavier. Presto.

Ex. 9

Lalo Symphonie Espagnole. Andante.

Ex. 10

Even in the case of 'time-honoured' fingerings as in the Paganini D Major Concerto

Ex. 11

and the Tchaikovsky Concerto

Ex. 12

I still favour the lower fingerings.

49

In the first Bartók Rhapsody (first movement, at No. 12), I play

Ex. 13

because: (*a*) third position would involve change of string on a semi-tone; (*b*) second position would give four notes to the D string, whereas my fingering gives three notes each to the three strings.

These changes of string on semitones are less noticeable in swift and *sautillé* passages like the following one from the Finale of the Mendelssohn Concerto, but they are to be avoided even in such cases.

Ex. 14

If we play it in the first position, we get the undesirable

Ex. 15

between the first and second bars. In addition we forgo the differentiation in tone colour on the two repeated F sharps which good articulation demands. Playing in the third position (Joachim) on the other hand gives it a darker colouring, somewhat out of character, and involves us in the swift change between the two F sharps

Ex. 16

As so often, the second position is the best solution.
    It gives us the chordal lay-out of:

Ex. 17

and preserves the good articulation between the two F sharps more comfortably.
    It goes without saying that in the descending chromatic scale (fourth and fifth bars) we should avoid the

Ex. 18

and the

Ex. 19

by adhering to the rule of stopped instead of open strings whenever possible (also in the ascending chromatic scale). This long-winded description of proceeding by *elimination* is—I think—necessary if the student is to be encouraged to think and decide for himself, sometimes in opposition to the printed page.

CHAPTER 12

STRESSES THE IMPORTANCE OF

tone colour, that is: the need to respect the composer's directions as to the string to be used, even at the price of discomfort. Hence to some examples where the exact opposite is suggested: namely the use of open strings for the sake of comfort!

ONCE THE student has conditioned his ear—that is, his sense of tone colour—he will find innumerable passages in his repertoire the fingerings of which (some of them by well-known editors!) will no longer satisfy him. This is as it should be.

The player should cultivate a seismograph-like sensitivity to brusque changes of tone colour caused by fingerings based on expediency and comfort rather than the composer's manifest or probable intentions. Almost any contemporary work will show how particular composers generally are about the use of certain strings for certain intended effects (*il suo proposto effetto*, as Beethoven expressed it). Thus, the fact that the masters of the past did not mark their scores with the same unequivocal precision as did, for instance, Bartók, is no excuse for playing the manifestly D string theme of the *tempo di Menuetto* of Beethoven's Op. 30, No. 3, marked in all available editions IIIza (that is, on the D string):

Ex. 1

with the lower fingering which calls into play both the D and G strings, thereby weakening Beethoven's *proposto effetto* of a serenely, horizontally flowing D string theme.

Obviously it is more difficult this way (especially the *crescendo* leading to the *sforzando* on E flat) but the violinist will have the satisfaction of having met a challenge instead of dodging it. The same player would scruple to disregard Bartók's command in the 1922 Sonata No. 1 first movement to play

Ex. 2

and in the second movement

Ex. 3

first on the A string, then repeat it on the D string. Why then this 'double standard' in ignoring *implied* exigencies by the masters of former centuries?

After having delivered myself of all this, I am now going to contradict myself by saying that in certain swift passages, interpolated open strings, *even* if they concern semitones on different strings (which I have tried in the preceding pages to present as highly undesirable!) can render us good service. An accompaniment figure like this one in the first movement of Schubert's G minor Sonatina, Op. 137, No. 3, which played in the first position involves us in awkward changes of the bow, can be made smoother by appropriate fingerings that may seem rather unorthodox:

Ex. 4

and so will the corresponding passage in the same first movement. In the Mozart–Kreisler Rondo

Ex. 5

the interpolated open A will take us smoothly from second to first position and give us variety on the three A's. Of course it can be played either in second or in first position, but there seems to me an advantage in avoiding the co-ordinating pitfall of

Ex. 6

in any form: whether as 1014 or as 4343 or as 1010 or as 3232. (There are more than enough co-ordinating challenges in this Rondo as it is!) The same challenge has to be faced in the 'Rondo to end all Rondos' (as it has been called) of the great Mozart K. 526 A major Sonata, where I find that any 'respite' from those

Ex. 7

figures must be taken advantage of, even if they involve us in open string semitone 'trespassing'!

Ex. 8

The Flesch fingering is rather too difficult in this Presto tempo and the *Urtext* (G. Henle) has a similarly unrealistic fingering (see above). I help myself with the expedient marked, just as I do at the beginning of the passage, four bars before, with similar expedients. It is a matter of sometimes abdicating a 'principle' in favour of a worthy cause. In Beethoven's Sonata Op. 30, No. 3 the *sforzandi* in the Rondo are so important that in order to give them the advantage of the G string it is worth while resorting to this expedient:

Ex. 9

And at the very end of the first movement of the 'Kreutzer' Sonata, I play the stormy passage:

Ex. 10

divided between the G and A strings in order to ensure the full impact of the sudden *forte* on the upbeat. The swift change of the bow from G to A string has to be negotiated so expertly that the listener should not even be aware of the unorthodox procedure. In some cases this playing of adjoining repeated figures on two strings (as in the Beethoven Op. 30, No. 3 excerpt above) gives the passage added spice, due to the enhanced dissonance: semitone steps played on two strings are more characteristic and dissonant than when played on the same string.

In the Tchaikovsky *Scherzo* Op. 42, No. 2 this is very apparent:

Ex. 11

And now to close this section dealing with the change of strings on semitones, I will set down my speculations about the simple descending G major scale in the Beethoven G major Romance at the risk of being accused of hair-splitting, of wasting printer's ink and reader's time. The obvious and comfortable third position I discarded right away (fingering (a)):

Ex. 12

because the three notes on the E string, and four each on the three other strings with the identical change of strings on

Ex. 13

did not satisfy my wish for variety, for asymmetry, for the *parlando* character that I feel, even in a scale, in such a context. The second and first position I found slightly better, but still monotonously symmetrical with sequences like

Ex. 14

Here are my reasons for fingering (b): five notes on the E string which was the 'spokesman' of the preceding bars anyway, three on the A string, four on the D string and three on the G string before starting the ascending chromatic scale leading us back to the E string theme.

It can also be played with fingering (c), which again gives us the advantage of unequal numbers of notes on each string and in addition a differentiation of colour between the two D's. If all this elicits from some readers an exclamation of 'much ado about nothing', I won't mind.

In the Rondo of Mozart's K. 526 Sonata that I mentioned a few paragraphs back, we can find an interesting example of a 'normal' first position fingering that we all, the Flesch and the Henle editions, etc., have accepted unquestioningly in spite of the bowing 'hardship' it entails.

Ex. 15

Play it in the third position and the bow jump from E to G string will have been avoided and a more appropriate darker tone colour gained.

CHAPTER 13

TRIES TO DISSUADE VIOLINISTS
from playing identical repeated notes with the same finger
by giving numerous examples from Beethoven, Mozart,
Mendelssohn, Max Bruch, César Franck and others

THE ANSWER to the question why we should whenever possible avoid playing two consecutive identical notes with the same finger is so self-evident that it is almost embarrassing for me to 'prove' my point by giving a few examples out of the innumerable ones that come to mind.

But when one sees how often we violinists fail to take advantage of what our instrument offers us, that is, the expressive enhancement that the naturally changed *timbre,* changed *vibrato*, infinitesimally changed intonation, of another finger can give, one is once again faced with the necessity of saying what really 'goes without saying'.

If any self-respecting pianist quite naturally and unquestioningly changes fingers on successive identical notes on his percussive and essentially unyielding instrument, how much more should *we* do so on ours that responds to every ever so slight variation of finger or bow pressure?

First let us dispose of those cases where even the most insensitive player will not fail to respond to the musical idea and change fingers on a repeated note, as in the *Larghetto* of the Beethoven Concerto:

Ex. 1

Joachim advocates the second G as a harmonic on the G string but hardly any interpreter today would follow him in this.

Another case where it is practically impossible not to respond to the implications of the composer's text is in the first movement of the César Franck Sonata:

Ex. 2

But if the student does not consciously cultivate a sensibility which will inhibit the tendency (based on our love of comfort!) to play repeated notes with the same finger, he may end up by using in Bach's Violin–Clavier Sonata No. 3 in the third movement the third and first positions instead of oing back and forth between the second and first positions, thus ensuring that each triplet segment can be played without change of string.

In the *Andante* of the Mendelssohn Concerto

Ex. 3

the expressiveness of the phrase is dependent on just these changes of fingers, and in the Rondo of the Beethoven Sonata Op. 30, No. 3, I try to give the four repeated syncopated F sharps added zest by playing each of them with changed fingers, thus:

Ex. 4

(and this without its having caused any undue 'hardship' as it brings me effortlessly to the fifth position).

59

Beethoven in the *Adagio cantabile* of the Sonata Op. 30, No. 2 clearly indicates his expressive intent by the *crescendo* and the *sforzando* on the third E flat.

Ex. 5

The change of finger on the *sf.* will help us realize this. His trio Op. 1, No. 3 will yield several similar cases: In the first movement, I play:

Ex. 6

In the *Andante cantabile* I use this fingering at the end:

Ex. 7

In the Beethoven Trio Op. 70, No. 1—first movement:

Ex. 8

and last movement:

Ex. 9

these fingerings come to me quite naturally.

Elsewhere in this book (in the section concerning bowing procedures) I speak of the second movement of the Handel D major Sonata. This example also serves the purpose of demonstrating the benefits of changing fingers on succeeding identical notes:

Ex. 10

In the first edition of the Max Bruch G minor Concerto we find few fingerings, but there is one that we may assume to be Joachim's, since the work was dedicated to him and probably seen by him in proof sheets. It is:

Ex. 11

The statement of the theme of the *Adagio* in the same concerto is mostly on the D string and I find in my music the notation in the sixth and seventh bars for this finger changing that I apparently already used over sixty years ago:

Ex. 12

Admittedly all this came more naturally to players who considered the E major Etude by Kreutzer

Ex. 13

with greater respect than their opposite numbers do today, and for whom Wieniawski's D minor Concerto with its:

Ex. 14

also in the last movement of the Wieniawski:

Ex. 15

and Vieuxtemps (*Ballade et Polonaise*) with its:

Ex. 16

so reminiscent of the italianate *cliché* we often find in L. Spohr's Concerto:

Ex. 17

were essential equipment for repertoire current at the turn of the century. A phrase like:

Ex. 18

in Viotti's beautiful A minor Concerto made the student soon conscious of the musical value of such fine points as the different tone colour of these crotchets

Ex. 19

and also conscious of the necessity of devoting himself time and again to this Kreutzer Etude! After all, the Kreutzer pattern

Ex. 20

will prove essential when we attempt to play this passage in the first movement of Mozart's D major Concerto, K. 218:

Ex. 21

and this should be the moment to pay a grateful tribute to Kreutzer's memory! . . . The student should realize that this Kreutzer Etude is in the main a *contraction* exercise, that is: material for the study of descending from a higher position to a lower one, by means of the contraction of the hand in 1–3, 1–4, or 2–4.

It is the freedom which this technique gives that will enable us to cope with a passage like

Ex. 22

in the first movement of the Brahms Concerto and with the *fiorituras* in the second movement of Bartók's Second Concerto.

Ex. 23

CHAPTER 14

DISCUSSES THE REASONS FOR THE NEGLECT
of a work like Schumann's A minor Sonata and incidentally
censures music publishers for reprinting inadequate editions
of eighty and more years ago. It also suggests that we sing,
hum, whistle in a better tempo than we play

IN USING editions of classical and romantic music, the date of the 'revision' (which, alas, can rarely be ascertained but can be more or less surmised) should be borne in mind. When, for instance, the editor of an edition of Schumann's A minor Sonata going back probably to the 1880s gives the beginning with the fingering

Ex. 1

we will do well to remember that in those days our $_{3\text{-}32}^{CFE}$ and, in fact, any whole-tone slide which we use now constantly would have been considered taboo (and fingerings involving the second, fourth, or half-positions something to be studiously avoided).

To give one example: twenty-one bars from the end of the first movement of this Schumann Sonata the editor of those days had no compunction about semitone shifts back and forth (in the coda, first movement), or in the lovely interlude in F minor (second movement) about fingerings of such primitiveness:

Ex. 2

but would have considered fingering the coda passage in the second position rather extravagant and playing the F minor example on the D string unnecessary.

(In the *Adagio* of Bach's G minor Solo Sonata for the same interval of a fourth (with which the Schumann Sonata opens) I use, of course, the 3–4 fingering which is suitable in Bach but less so in Schumann.

Ex. 3

It always seems to me that we have an analogy there with changes in the 'usage' of language.)

When thinking of this beautiful work of Schumann's—nowadays alas, neglected—I often ask myself whether its neglect is not due to some extent to the failure of violinists to cope with some of its unviolinistic aspects. Take that slow 'fast' movement, marked *Lebhaft* (*vivo*) and ♩ = 94: what control of the bow arm is needed in order to play it at the prescribed 'slow' pace; how much easier it is to adopt a faster tempo, but how much this essentially Schumannesque inspiration loses in the process! Part of the bowing difficulty lies in the counter-clockwise movements of the bow if played in the first position:

Ex. 4

But play it mostly in the second position and use extensions as in

Ex. 5

and the bow problem will to a great extent disappear. It is often the unwillingness of the executant to meet a challenge, to find a solution to a difficulty, that makes him declare that the study of a certain composition is not worth while. But let him experiment, let him try and bring out latent possibilities in a neglected work like the Schumann A minor Sonata and he will change his mind. Small things like this fingering in the admittedly not rousing third movement

Ex. 6

can enhance its effectiveness.

Looking through some editions of neglected masterpieces, I cannot help feeling that the neglect stems to a certain extent from the practice of some publishers who entrust editions to violinists who have never played these works in public and then keep these inadequate editions in print for decades because of economic expediency. No wonder then that the student is discouraged when sight-reading such a work and his teacher similarly discouraged in having to mark the copy 'from scratch'.

One publishing firm with the prestige of a century's activity still continues to reprint editions of violin works made (presumably around 1870 or 1880) by a pedagogue born in 1822, who died in 1907. It is easy to imagine that such bowings and fingerings show their age today.

On the other hand, when publishers entrust an edition to some prominent violinist of today, he often fails to give us his fingerings and bowings precisely at a place where the student needs them most! If he feels a reluctance to commit himself to one solution, he should give alternatives. To 'improvise' fingerings that will stand the test of public performance is, in the case of an unviolinistic but engrossing work like this Schumann Sonata, well-nigh impossible.

Add to these obstacles the elusiveness of its idiom, the cross accents, stresses on the last quaver in a 'con passione' 6/8 tempo (something that Brahms remembered when writing the D minor Sonata Op. 108), the stresses on the weak beats in the lovely second movement—by my count twenty-one in this short piece!—and one will not be surprised at the unwillingness of teacher, student, and glamorous virtuoso to face such a challenge. One editor, in despair at what he calls Schumann's ineffective handling of the two instruments, simply redistributes the parts.

As the prestige of Schumann at the time of writing is at a comparatively low ebb (especially with violinists, who are notoriously—let us say—uninterested in a composer's œuvre as a whole), let me remind them that Alban Berg devoted an essay of twelve pages to an analysis of Schumann's *Träumerei,* a little piece of twenty-four bars. (True, it is not only an analysis, but a refutation of the gushing literary manner of 'interpretation' and 'appreciation' and a working model of how an inspired melody can be followed step by step.)

If we turn from the third movement of the Schumann, with its ♩=94 pace to the second movement of the Debussy Sonata: *Fantasque et léger* marked ♩=75, we find a similar challenge of bow control due to the relatively slow 'controlled' *spiccato* the composer demands.

(Isn't the Schumann Finale too, *fantasque et léger*? In my own practising, I go from one example to the other, just playing fragments from each, trying to impress upon myself similarities of mood and of procedure.) The tempo that is, alas, too often adopted for this elusive and demanding second movement is too fast and in contradiction to Debussy's metronome marking (and his modifications of tempo: ♩=75, with some slight *stringendos* and *meno mossos* and a considerable slowing down in the last six bars). This forces me to make the following unorthodox statement. We (myself included) too often adopt tempi that are *in contradiction with our own convictions*! In this case, for instance, we fail, because the controlled *spiccato* is simply too much of an ordeal to a bow-arm used to the faster, more comfortable, 'uncontrolled' *spiccato*!

It is my conviction that we often compromise tempo-wise, according to our technical equipment: we play fast when this comes easier to us, we play too slowly when this flatters our innate tendencies, our tone production, for instance. While I have not been able to adhere strictly to Debussy's ♩=75, I think I managed to come fairly near to it in my three recordings with Bartók, Foldes and Roy Bogas, and in my many live performances.

Albert Schweitzer already remarked upon this tendency in his Bach biography, written some sixty-five years ago, when he said that Bach's *Andantes* are generally played too slowly and the *Allegros* too fast. It really amounts to this: it is our instrumental idiosyncrasies that too often determine our tempi. That is why we 'think' and sing (or rather: hum, or whistle, or grunt) a movement away from our instrument often more correctly than when we play it.

Conductors have this advantage over us: I have seen one of our great ones sit at his table away from the piano, pocket score and metronome before him and he—decides. . . .

CHAPTER 15

DEMONSTRATES THE ADVANTAGES OF
an 'open' left hand after an excursion into elementary pedagogics quite unbecoming to a book of this kind but illustrated by digressions that range from Kreutzer to Bartók and Hindemith

I KNOW I am not drawing attention to anything very new in discussing the 'natural' tendency of the violinist to play sharp with the first finger in certain keys:

Ex. 1

But most authorities persist in perpetuating the myth of the 'natural' finger position of a fourth span:

Ex. 2

and this forces me to touch upon the question. It seems to me, that this tendency of the first finger to play sharp in certain contexts is caused by the pampering of the beginner's hand in the early stages of tuition, when even the augmented fourth, for instance:

Ex. 3

is studiously avoided, instead of conditioning the novice's hand right from the beginning to a fan-like opening of—even a young child's small hand.

In my—admittedly minority—opinion the

Ex. 4

position is no more 'natural' than the

Ex. 5

or even the position of the hand in the stretch of a fifth is 'unnatural'.

Ex. 6

As early as 1910 Ferdinand Küchler already spoke of half-position

Ex. 7

being identical with the '*tiefe*' (low) I position

Ex. 8

calling

Ex. 9

the 'normal' I position

Ex. 10

the 'raised' I position

Ex. 11

the 'low' II position

Ex. 12

the 'normal' II position and so on.

In his Tabulation he did not hesitate to include the whole-tone sequence

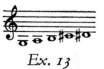

Ex. 13

even though his Method was destined for beginners. On the other hand, in the 1905 Joachim–Moser Method, Andreas Moser considered an augmented fourth 'too difficult' for a beginner and for this reason advocated the study of the C major scale much later. In this he followed no less an authority than Viotti (1821).

To return to this question of what is 'natural' and what 'unnatural', let a well-trained violinist of habitually good intonation drop his four fingers in an inert, sluggish, that is *'natural'* manner and he will see by this test what an illusory concept this 'natural' falling of the fingers in the 'right' place is! The fingers will *not* fall 'naturally' into the pattern of whole and half tones, whatever that pattern may be: whether a sequence in a major or minor key or in whole tones.

I would not have ventured into these realms of elementary pedagogy, which may seem out of place in the opinion of the advanced students and their teachers who may be among my readers, if I did not feel that our whole contemporary outlook on fingering is closely bound up with extensions, the bridging of the different positions by intermediate *'en route'* procedures and the like.

Fingered octaves which Auer traces back to Wilhelmj (1845–1908), that is, to the 1870s, and which in fact are based on the extended position of the hand, have had a liberating influence on our fingering habits. (We must remember that the seventeenth Caprice of Paganini with its C minor middle section, which nowadays is taught and performed exclusively in fingered octaves, was still published with the traditional 1/4 fingering when I started studying the Caprices in 1904. My copy was edited by Edmund Singer (1830–1912), well-known teacher of Hungarian origin—like Joachim, Leopold Auer and Joseph Böhm (1795–1876)—who taught Joachim, Singer and Ernst.)

A glimpse at editions of sixty to seventy years ago (some of them still being used today) gives a good idea of the 'then' and 'now'. The chord of

Ex. 14

was changed to

Ex. 15

73

in many editions of the A minor Solo Sonata of Bach because of the

Ex. 16

stretch, despite the fact that Bach's contemporary Johann Georg Pisendel (1687–1755) demands extensions like

Ex. 17

and stretches of tenths in his fine A minor Solo Sonata and Bach in the Chaconne

Ex. 18

in the E major Prelude and elsewhere:

Ex. 19

The trill section of Tartini's Devil's Trill Sonata is also based on the weird effect of the unison-stretch

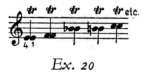

Ex. 20

and its *Allegro* contains such unison effects as

Ex. 21

and

Ex. 22

It is significant that the Joachim–Moser (1905) edition evades the issue and does not print this 'essential' fingering, which practically all editions (i.e. Fr. Hermann, Kreisler, Hubay) carry.

Of course the change-over in the nineteenth century from the short neck and short string-length of the seventeenth- and eighteenth-century violin to the instrument as we now know it had something to do with the reluctance of nineteenth-century editors to cope with extensions and unisons. These were easier to do on the short-neck violin, but the general use of fingered octaves in our own day and on our own lengthened violin-neck has made us aware that if the hand is 'opened up', we can very well adapt ourselves to this usage.

R. Kreutzer in his nowadays practically unknown nineteen Etudes-Caprices (Ricordi Edition, 2482) devoted No. 15 to a '*bariolage*' Etude that starts like this:

Ex. 23

75

and goes on to the unison:

Ex. 24

that take the student from the first to the sixth position.

Kreutzer published these nineteen Etudes early in the nineteenth century and it is obvious that the great teacher was already then conscious of the need for what I have called the 'opening up' of the hand. Editors around the turn of the century were unwilling to take advantage of the benefits of the 'liberation' I have mentioned and this is responsible for many anomalies in our fingering habits.

Without even going into the question of the use of tenths it is noticeable how indispensable the unison fingerings are to an 'opening up' of our left hand. The Cadenza in the first movement of the Mendelssohn Concerto is surely a modest enough technical 'demand' measured by the technical requirements of other works in our repertoire, but this passage precisely took this unison hand position for granted. Hubay considered the doubling or appoggiatura-like touching of the F sharp indispensable* since the movement of the G string basses demands this:

Ex. 25

* In this edition (Rozsnyai), now out of print, Hubay notates:

while the score has:

76

Words need not be wasted on the advantage of the unison and fingered octave position in moving across the fingerboard by easy stages. Beethoven, too, took this truly 'natural' open hand position for granted when he marked the theme of the Finale of the Op. 127 Quartet '*sul G*'.

Ex. 26

It is probably these advantages of the 'unison' hand position that Paul Hindemith had in mind when he wrote the *Saitenwechsel* (change of strings) Exercise in the 1926 *Studies for Violinists* (published by Schott—alas—only thirty years later!). The exercise is actually built on this hand position; it starts with:

Ex. 27

gives sequences like:

Ex. 28

and in his 'Exercise across the position without change of position' demonstrates what he means by his somewhat puzzling title by writing:

Ex. 29

77

The composer, in the Foreword written in 1956, says: 'These pieces reflect my own way of playing in past years'; a page like this one from the Coda of his Solo Sonata Op. 31, No. 2, is no doubt greatly enhanced by idiomatic fingerings like the following, which most of the time dispense with shifts altogether.

Ex. 30

Bartók, by the way, uses the 'unison' position of Hindemith's *Saitenwechsel* Exercises in the third movement of his Fourth Quartet (1928) in the following passage for the first violin:

Ex. 31

In the passage from Bach's C minor Sonata for clavier and violin:

Ex. 32

and in the last movement of Prokofiev's Second Concerto changes of position can be dispensed with altogether:

78

Ex. 33

I cannot resist the temptation of devising a further extension of this design, descending by easy stages without the jerky changes of position in the Sevčik manner. Incidentally, this will give the student who reads these pages a working model of how to free himself from printed, 'ready-made' exercises and how to procure himself the luxury of the 'hand-tailored' ones during practice hours. . . .

Ex. 34

Such exercises are preferable to sterile discussions and demonstrations concerning the role of the left thumb in shifting. We have seen that composers always seem to anticipate technical developments decades ahead; teaching in the meanwhile jogs along in the old ruts in leisurely fashion, unconscious of 'things to come'.

CHAPTER 16

DRAWS ATTENTION TO THE EMANCIPATION
we owe to fingered octaves, mentions in passing the 'Geminiani
grip' and Bartók's pattern of fourths, harks back to
Chapter 12 à propos of tone colour and the judicious
choice of strings, speaks about so-called 'crab-fingerings'
and ends—unexpectedly— on a hopeful note

WHENEVER I complain to another violinist that we are 'tradition-ridden in the matter of fingering' or 'reluctant to open up our hand' in the unison position (for instance, B flat on the A string with the first finger and the same note with the fourth finger on the D string), in short, whenever I point out vestiges of these 'pre-fingered-octave' habits in our editions, I hear disclaimers. No violinist I speak to seems to be guilty, in playing, of these old-fashioned habits.

How is it, then, that not one of the many editions of the Beethoven Concerto has so much as hinted at the possibility of a fingered-octave solution to those redoubtable D minor and D major octave runs in the first movement? To my knowledge, my 1963 edition (Curci, Milan) is the first to suggest such unorthodoxy. Tests I have made have fully convinced me and my 'guinea-pigs' (chosen from among the less gifted, technically speaking) of the efficacy of this approach.

Or take the triplet variation in the same movement, which players of my generation used to struggle with, because the conventional first and fourth finger octaves remained such a die-hard tradition. In my fingered octave suggestion the only real difficulty remains the jump of a fifth between D and A (second and third finger), but the menacing one between G and C with the fourth finger has been replaced by the relatively comfortable one with the third and fourth finger. (It is unnecessary to remind the reader of the discomfort the gradual diminishing of the fingerboard causes in the upper reaches, if played with traditional 1 and 4 fingering).

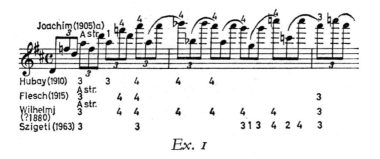

Ex. 1

Another case in point is the passage in octaves in the Rondo at the third entry of the Rondo theme, where Joachim, Wilhelmj, Hubay and Flesch prescribe the traditional fingering, while I suggest ending it (one bar before the resumption of the theme) with:

Ex. 2

Granted that the sliding first finger from

Ex. 3

is somewhat uncomfortable, still the fingered octaves make the ascent on the whole less perilous.

It is enlightening to compare the two editions Carl Flesch published of the Mendelssohn Concerto. In the first one (probably 1910–12) the proverbially perilous dominant seventh octave passage in the first movement was meant to be tackled in the traditional way, with first and fourth finger

81

octaves. In the second version (1927) Flesch advocates fingered octaves. (I adopt a different sequence of fingers, which only goes to prove the fluidity of all such solutions.)

Ex. 4

Those of us who have 'lived dangerously' with the old fingering for decades should not, of course, attempt this change-over. But young players can and should experiment with it. They will see that the passage gains in boldness and thrust through the *legato-* link of the long bow *détaché* octaves (akin to the bowing used in the Kreisler (Pugnani) Prelude) by avoiding the stoppings of the bow between each stroke.

I should add that the choice between conventional, first and fourth finger, and fingered octaves need not be absolute; one can change from one to the other and back again at any point in an ascending or descending passage.

The opening of the Mendelssohn Concerto is, I think, an interesting illustration of the change in our fingering *'mores'*. Joachim, who played it under the composer's direction in 1846, marks the opening in his 1905 edition as starting in the first position and uses harmonics three times on the

Ex. 5

(in the first solo). By about 1920, Flesch advocates starting in the second position, but—significant concession!—puts the formerly traditional first position in brackets, discards the harmonics on the

Ex. 6

82

(presumably because by then gut E strings were no longer being used) and avoided Joachim's

Ex. 7

by advocating the stretched (lower) procedure. The fact that in the third bar from the beginning, Flesch enjoins the student (in a footnote) to play

Ex. 8

'without *glissando*', shows that even as recently as Flesch's time a distance of a sixth was considered an occasion for a *glissando* possibly even with a *Hilfsnote*

Ex. 9

in between. Tabulations like these are admittedly long winded but show how slowly new concepts emerge in our craft, which in a previous book I called 'tradition-ridden'.

Although the following excerpt from a Mozart Quartet (K. 590) cannot be called perilous or redoubtable (like the Beethoven and Mendelssohn ones) it is—I think—a neat illustration of the advantages a comfortably spread-out left hand can bring us.

Ex. 10

The passage in octaves in the coda of the Finale of the Brahms Concerto

Ex. 11

is one that those who start with a 'clean slate' will have little trouble in learning with my suggested fingerings. This will *not* be the case with those who have tried the traditional 1 and 4 fingering! It is not only difficult passages like the above that can be made easier but simple ones like the following one from the first movement of the Beethoven Concerto that can gain in smoothness by adopting more rational fingerings than those of the past:

Ex. 12

It is the unison B (1st and 4th) and the use of the half position (second bar) that solve the problem. This smooth joining together of adjacent positions is at the very root of the problems posed by some contemporary works like the Second Bartók Concerto or the Sonata No. 1 (1923). Once one has recognized the basic pattern, everything falls into place, but try and play these with traditional fingerings and they become forbidding.

To return to the question of 'natural' versus 'unnatural' stretched basic positions on our fingerboard—after these several digressions—it is interesting to find the so-called 'Geminiani grip'

Ex. 13

(1751) in Bartók's Rhapsody No. 1 (1928) transposed one tone higher two bars before No. 6.

Ex. 14

It is interesting not only from the violinistic-technical point of view, but also as a sign of Bartók's preoccupation with the interval of a fourth (see the principal theme of his Concerto No. 2).

Ex. 15

In the example from Rhapsody No. 1 the fourths involve no change of position, but generally fourths are a help in bridging over positions smoothly, as for instance in this passage from the Bartók Sonata No. 1 (1923).

Ex. 16

In the following passage from the first movement of the Bartók Concerto No. 2 we find a preponderance of steps of fourths:

Ex. 17

and these will lead the student to some fingering (not necessarily mine!) that brings his hand down in easy stages. But it is important to recognize the salient pattern first.

Ex. 18

At bar 251 (in the same movement), I find a 'basic' fifth position (with modifications involving the fourth and third positions) easier and better sounding than the obvious first position.

In bars 371–2, I favour the identical pattern 1.2.3.4. on account of the well-defined succession of the strings; two groups on the G, one on the D, two on the A, one on the E string; but using the low positions is also a workable solution.

When Bartók (in Rhapsody No. 1) writes:

Ex. 19

he is not in the least conscious of making undue demands on the stretching capacities of the violinist's hand. Rather it is old-fashioned fingerings like Joachim's in the Mozart Concerto (K. 218) that are unreasonable. He writes:

Ex. 20

86

when the lower fingering takes us comfortably and safely down to the third position.

Now a digression: I try to keep apart the different segments of a theme by confining, whenever possible, each one to one of the four strings. The passage in the development section in the first movement of the Mendelssohn Concerto is to my mind a particularly telling example of the 'naturalness' of such procedures:

Ex. 21

In using the G, D and A strings for our three thematic segments and asking the first violins of the orchestra to complete this soaring long phrase on the E string (by falling in on the F sharp on the E string and on no account in the 'expedient' 3rd position), we will have 'fulfilled' our wonderful instrument; the violin, with its four so eloquently different strings. . . .

In a passage of this kind the choice of string may be conscious or subconscious in the mind of the composer. He may more often than not omit to specify his wishes; he may take for granted what later editors and performers will fail to see.

This came to my mind recently, when, playing the Menuetto (*Allegro*) of Schubert's A minor Sonatina Op. 132, No. 2, I realized that the Menuetto proper can (and should) be played on the two lower strings, thus leaving its Trio entirely to the colouring of the two upper strings. How important this 'unwritten' wish of a composer of genius can be, will be apparent when we first play the movement (Menuetto and Trio) in the first position, using the G, D and A strings, thus not respecting the keeping apart of Menuetto and Trio, 'instrumentationwise': lower strings for Menuetto, upper strings for Trio, and later comparing this way of least resistance with the procedure I suggest! It is up to us to detect these unwritten (and sometimes perhaps even unconscious) wishes of the composer.

Let the student devise his own fingerings on the basis of the following *schema*: first two bars: G string; third bar: D; bars 4–7: fourth and fifth position; bars 8–12: fourth and third position. Second section: start in fourth position and stay throughout on D and G strings; last six bars on G only.

We will find similar coincidences between a musical idea and its execution on a given string or strings, or, rather, in a given tone colour, in the two other Schubert Sonatinas too. I play the Menuetto, *Allegro Vivace* of the G minor in the fourth position, on the G and D strings, in order to achieve the contrast of the flowing E flat Trio that is 'meant' principally for the two upper strings. In the Andante of the D major Sonatina I use the G string entirely for the theme (A major) in order to set off the one in A minor, that naturally falls to the A and D strings. The radius of the theme in A major is

Ex. 22

that in A minor

Ex. 23

I am quite conscious of the disfavour into which the romantic slides on intervals of a sixth have fallen in recent years,

Ex. 24

but this disfavour on the part of adherents of the *Neue Sachlichkeit* should not deter us from doing justice to the typically Mendelssohnian romantic-

88

ism of these singing, soaring phrases. Playing these sixths 'in the position' with 3–4 or 2–3 fingering—in my biased opinion—clips the wings of the phrase. (At the risk of repeating what I wrote in a previous book of mine: I always deplore the unwillingness of violinists to face the challenge of playing the beautiful *Adagio* opening of Mozart's G major (K. 216) Concerto on the E string for which it was so obviously meant, and playing it instead in the 'convenient' fifth position.)

On the other hand this variation from the Vitali Chaconne

Ex. 25

is an example of how a succession of slides can be avoided, something that is specially desirable in sequential phrases like this one. But one could endlessly go on giving such examples and at the finish one might seem to be crashing through open gates, for I know many readers will already have been in agreement with the implication of these last few pages.

The reader will have noticed that a great deal in the preceding pages is aimed at the old straitjacket-like concept of playing in positions and at the unjustified privileges that the first and third positions came to usurp in our fingering habits. We are now well on the way to a more rational outlook, which allows us to take advantage of 'in-between' positions, allows us to avoid jerky changes, benefits us in effecting these changes by easy stages. When between 1917 and 1924, I taught the *'classe de virtuosité'* at the Geneva Conservatoire (where one of my predecessors had been Henri Marteau), I already started fighting antiquated fingering habits and coined the word 'crab-fingerings', for these 'in-between' position passages. This word is now being changed into 'crawl' and 'creeping' by teachers who follow the laudable trend these days and this is all to the good. It is not the designation that matters, but what it stands for.

Trends (and in fact 'inventions') start by being in the air—as it were—and then emerge gradually (and simultaneously) in several areas, so there can be no question of priority claims. This process is still going on and—I hope—will continue to go on.

CHAPTER 17

OUTLINES THE AUTHOR'S SUGGESTIONS
for overcoming an intonation pitfall

I AM conscious that what I am about to do is something that I intensely dislike in books by colleagues: that is, to propose an 'infallible' formula for some chink in the violinist's armour! But colleagues and pupils, to whom I have in the past pointed out the 'short cut' that is to follow, have persuaded me that it is new (if anything can be new in our domain!) and that it works; so here I am joining the ranks of those I look upon with disfavour.

This short-cut concerns consecutive sixths, thirds and other intervals played with the same pair of fingers. Every teacher and pupil has suffered from lapses of intonation due to the alternation of whole-tones with semi-tones in one part or the other.

(From now on in the next few pages I will mark semitones with $\wedge$,

whole tones with $\overline{}$ signs.)

In this passage from Max Bruch's Op. 26, for instance,

Ex. 1

the semitone step on the D string is likely to be too wide, the B flat sharp and the A natural flat; and the whole tone step, D to C on the G string, will be correspondingly out of tune in one of many ways.

If you play any scale in sixths or thirds (or, of course, tenths!) you will feel the same insecurity due to the necessity of reconciling whole tone steps in one part with the semitone-steps in the other:

Ex. 2

When both parts move in identical steps like $^{\text{C}}_{\text{A flat}} - ^{\text{D}}_{\text{B flat}}$, we feel secure. Here is another example:

Ex. 3

The reason for this is simply that the player (and correspondingly, the hand) is not 'conscious' of when and where these simultaneous contradictions between wide and narrow placing of the fingers occur.

It is, however, better to test this difficulty (and my suggestion for overcoming it) on a few passages from the hundreds in our repertoire. In this, from the first movement of the Brahms Concerto,

Ex. 4

I prefer the $^{2\cdot2}_{4\cdot4}$ fingering in order to avoid the whole-tone step on $^{\text{F-E flat}}_{\text{D-C}}$ with $^{1\cdot1}_{3\cdot3}$. If we practise the difficult coda passage in the Finale of this Concerto analytically, that is:

Ex. 5

we encounter these unequal steps once again.

91

In the Finale of the Max Bruch G minor Concerto we find both thirds and tenths that demand our vigilance.

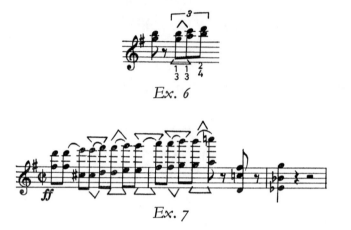

Ex. 6

Ex. 7

The middle section of the Andante of the Mendelssohn Concerto has these unequal steps,

Ex. 8

and the Kreisler (Pugnani) Allegro will probably give trouble to any violinist not conditioned to precisely this difficulty:

Ex. 9

We see that it is the sixths of the third and fourth fingers that 'pilot' the hand upwards. These sixths are successively major, minor, minor, major,

major, and so on—in confusing sequence! The difficulty is increased when the figure *descends* into the first position. In many chord sequences, this digital memory is indispensable. In the Paganini Caprice No. 11 we find this:

Ex. 10

in the Tartini–Léonard Sonata in G major (No. 3):

Ex. 11

and:

Ex. 12

We meet the same intonation problem as in the Tartini excerpts in the eighth variation of the Caprice No. 24 by Paganini:

Ex. 13

93

and in the Bach Brandenburg Concerto No. 4.

Ex. 14

Although the A major Caprice No. 21 by Paganini is mainly a study in sixths we are not faced with these alternate major and minor steps except in a few cases such as:

Ex. 15

and of course in the two scales with the same pair of fingers:

Ex. 16   *Ex. 17*

which the ambitious student should treat as a sort of 'gold standard' of the independence of the fingers in effecting whole tone and semitone steps at will.

Still another Paganini Caprice, No. 2, in B minor, confronts us with a further problem: how to achieve secure intonation in a passage which alternates between the G and E strings:

Ex. 18

This can be profitably practised in this way: by filling out the space between the two parts with chords, audibly or inaudibly. (I credit the student with sufficient knowledge of harmony to do this filling-in himself.)

Kreisler in his cadenza to the third movement of the Beethoven Concerto has a passage in semiquavers which presents various problems of a similar kind.

Tchaikovsky's Valse-Scherzo Op. 34 has a passage in fast *Allegro* tempo

Ex. *19*

which trips up all but the best-grounded players. It is the whole-tone step of the first finger and the necessity of playing the F sharp with a true leading note sharpness that causes this almost chronic intonation lapse.

The coda of the first movement of the Tchaikovsky Concerto has a passage that is characteristic of all that has been discussed in these last pages.

Ex. 20

In this example it is also the succession of fourths that needs special vigilance.

Ex. 21

Before I present my solution to all these problems, let me urge the student

(*a*) not to disregard the lifting of the bow in the first (Max Bruch) excerpt;

(*b*) to experiment with scales in sixths in different keys, but with *consecutive* (first and second, or second and third or third and fourth fingers) fingering; with scales in thirds of course and, if possible, fragments of scales in tenths.

(*c*) to expand the suggested Brahms Finale 'exercise' by going sequence-wise into the first position and—if sufficiently adventurous! applying this pattern to other keys as well.

(*d*) to make use of the tenths in the Bruch Finale excerpt for similar transposition adventures.

(*e*) to realize that the middle section of the Mendelssohn Andante is a gift to the student who knows how to expand technical problems with inventiveness, with that modest dose of creativity that all practise time should contain.

And after this attempt to track down and analyse the intonation difficulty of these and similar passages, my suggestion will come as an anti-climax in its utter simplicity. It is this: *focus your attention solely on the finger that is making the whole-tone step and disregard completely the finger that is making the semitone step.* (If *both* fingers travel across the same interval, then of course we divide our attention equally, as in octaves!) Let the semitone *fall into place by the action of the whole-tone finger.* It will!

Of course I must qualify this rather rash statement by making it clear that I am not claiming to insure the student against false intonation. What I mean is, that if the initial sixth, or third, or tenth is in tune and if the digital memory (for this particular passage) is sufficiently alert to 'know' in which part the whole tones lie, and if one can refrain from shifting about both fingers in haphazard fashion in an effort to correct the faulty intonation, then the battle is won and the semitones will *automatically* be in tune. We may consider it axiomatic that the finger making the whole-tone step drags what I may call the inert finger (making the semitone step) along with it.

Of course these 'ifs' are no small matter. Nor are they exhaustive. This patent medicine needs still more 'Directions For Use'. For instance, this one: the finger effecting the whole-tone step has to act swiftly, decisively. In practising, therefore, if it misses its goal (too sharp or too flat) it should never correct itself, but start again until the hand 'remembers' the distance and becomes foolproof, which is the dream of all of us. Only then shall we be sure of the semitone falling into place, as I have rashly promised.

This point can be demonstrated in a matter of minutes, but the explanation is necessarily lengthy. I include it because my colleagues and pupils have urged me to.

CHAPTER 18

DEVOTED TO BACH, AND THUS
the core of the book; just as Bach should be the
core of a violinist's life . . .

IF THESE pages open with the full text of one of the less demanding—
technically speaking!—homophonic Bach pieces, it is because I feel that a
'clinical' example, a piece seen from two angles (from that of a respected
master like Carl Flesch and from my own), may make the meaning of much
of what follows clearer. I refrain from overloading this musical example
with expression marks, such as cesuras, dynamic nuances and the like, nor
do I specify which parts of the bow are to be used. The few markings the
reader will find such as 'almost imperceptible stopping of the bow' and
'cesura (*Luftpause*)' are from the Flesch edition (Peters). Sound as these
markings are, I should have preferred to leave the student to discover them
for himself from an inner musical conviction and not in obedience to a
distinguished editor's injunction. My fingerings are suggestions only.

BACH: ALLEMANDE FROM THE D MINOR PARTITA

/ = almost imperceptible stopping of bow

// = cesura (Luftpause)

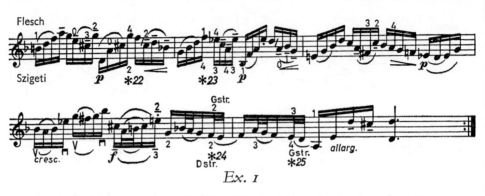

Ex. 1

1 Flesch doubles the upbeat D. (The MS. doubles only the downbeat D.)

2 Less grandiloquent than on G string. Equal tone colour. Three notes on G, three on D string.*

3 Avoidance of slide between D and A. Lies comfortably.

4 Avoidance of open A preceding the G.

5 More simple and straightforward.

6 Avoidance of G harmonic.

7 Avoidance of change of position between C and B.

8 The alternation between downbow and upbow is preferable to downbows on every strong beat.

9 Avoidance of the otherwise unavoidable clashing open A with the G sharp on the E string.

10 Avoidance of downbow on downbeats.

11 First position, greater simplicity.

12 Shift from third to first position undesirable.

13 Vibrate on D string on the A.

14 First position gives better voice-leading: G sharp to A on E string.

15 Avoidance of change of string on semitone (D to C sharp).

16 My fingering avoids third position to first position shift.

17 Change of tone colour on repeated segment.

18 First position more simple and straightforward.

19 Avoidance of 'leap' between E and D strings.

20 More logical phrasing—three notes on D string.

* *The student might well ask: Why start in fourth position and change to first position in the course of these two first bars?*

The answer is: staying in fourth position would yield four notes on G string and two on D string. Therefore better equilibrium if my suggestion is followed. Of course it could also be played in third position, but—to my mind—with less impact. (In my solution no fourth finger is used.) Another solution would be that by Adolf Busch, who starts in first position (fourth finger) and moves on to second position on the F.

100

21 Avoidance of harmonic A dear to nineteenth-century taste.
22 Greater simplicity.
23 More logical.
24 G string too grandiloquent.
25 Small stretch allows avoidance of shift between D and A.

No doubt the availability in recent years of *Urtexts* and facsimiles of some manuscripts (like those of the Bach Solo Sonatas) has brought us many insights and a degree of assurance in some doubtful cases. But it has also bred a type of 'know-all' who—armed with a photostat or a facsimile—will cry 'sacrilege' every time he meets with a trill that the composer did not mark in the manuscript, forgetting that such trills and other embellishments were taken for granted in his time and were, consequently, often not notated by the composer. They will also question, or protest against, any deviation from the solemn, ponderous tempi of the 'Victorian-organist' and the bowings that used to be considered in keeping with the style of every one of the three great Bach Violin Fugues. They will not admit that each of these is a law unto itself and that what is right for the G minor Fugue (in common time) will be out of place in the 'singing' flowing Fugue in C major, based on the Hymn *Komm, Heiliger Geist, Herre Gott* and that although the manuscript (as in many other cases) does not specify the *legato* enunciation of the theme

Ex. 2

the *détaché* reading that is sometimes used nowadays (see the examples by Capet and Flesch, Nos. 3 and 7) cannot invalidate a tradition that goes back to the executions and the editions of Ferdinand David (1810–73), Joachim, Hubay, and Adolf Busch.

The dissenting voices include Lucien Capet, who in his 1915 edition advocates playing the theme on the G string with an accent on each note (!) and moreover adds a sharp to the second F, saying that the sharp seems to have been omitted by Bach(!)

Ex. 3

J. Hellmesberger (1828–93) notates it thus:

Ex. 4

J. Champeil (1958), who has gone deeply into the question of the 'unequal lengths of notes',* and bases his findings on Quantz, George Muffat, Michel Corette and others, suggests this:

Ex. 5

Maglioni (and no doubt others) writes:

Ex. 6

And Flesch:

Ex. 7

* The French in the eighteenth century often intended short notes following longer dotted notes to be played shorter than their written value, e.g. a quaver following a dotted crotchet was played as a semi-quaver following a double-dotted crotchet.

I will not go into the 'merits of the case' of each one of these examples nor enumerate the reasons for my allegiance to the *legato* approach (F. David, Joachim, Hubay, Busch), but will only say this. The canon that follows leaves us in no doubt as to the necessity of a bowing that allows us to respect the letter and spirit of the upbeat instead of shortening it to half its value as in

Ex. 8

instead of:

Ex. 9

Likewise no blind follower of photostats can convince us that it is right to give the A minor Fugue a solemn *portato*, approximately $\mathbf{\downarrow} = 60$, just because the violin MS. does not show the slurs on the quavers in the second bar, which Bach's own version for clavier in D minor (Bach Gesellschaft Vol. XI, II), does show! The testimony of musicians like Joachim, Hellmesberger, Hubay, Capet, all of whom considered the

Ex. 10

approach as the valid one and some of whom even underlined the naturalness of the ♪♪ ♪♪ by adding the (unnecessary) phrasing indication of accents to make sure of the right articulation, should convince even the most fanatic of the 'guardians' of the *Urtext*.

When I advocate this approach instead of the unarticulated and contrast-less one, I of course postulate the greatest possible variety of bowing stresses within the framework of the basic ♪♪♪♪ ; an unrelieved ♪♪♪♪ of the same weight, same texture, played at the same part of the bow can bring to the listener the same *ennui* (or to paraphrase Alice: the 'same sameness'!) as an unrelieved ♪♪♪♪ .

We can create this diversity in unity now by stabbing the two upbow semiquavers fairly near to the nut, now by playing them lightly in the middle, by reverting sometimes to the ♪♪♪♪ but keeping the bouncy, buoyant character of the theme in evidence, playing them sometimes near the nut *balzato*, sometimes fanfare-like with 'normal' *détaché*; but above all by creating dialogues by playing for instance bars 18–23 in this way:

Ex. 11

and bars 24–29 somewhat more weightily, seriously, ♪♪♪♪♪♪ with 'basic' ♪♪♪♪♪ bowing, but giving the crotchets somewhat greater length, that is, more 'bow hair'.

It is like a throwback to the bad old days of J. Hellmesberger, in the 1880s, to see that Carl Flesch in 1930 'realized' Bach's descending crotchets in semiquavers, thus nullifying the effect Bach's symbolic notation made so abundantly clear.

Our vocabulary for the description of bowing procedures is woefully inadequate: *spiccato, détaché, martelé* can mean a great many things according to the part of the bow we use, according to the length of our strokes and so on. The word *spiccato* covers both the '*Moto perpetuo*' type and the heavy,

104

slow, biting variety appropriate to the coda of the first movement of the Tchaikovsky Concerto (to mention just one example). We have no single word to describe even that all-important articulation device, the short lifting of the bow towards the nut. Thus it is exceedingly difficult for me to give in the above sentences an idea of how to achieve the variety, the vividness that keeps the listener always on the alert for new happenings.

Bach's contemporary Johann Mattheson (1681–1764) wrote about precisely this A minor Fugue: 'Who would think that the nine short notes of the theme could be sufficient to produce a polyphonic composition of a sheet's length in a completely natural way and without any strange expansion?' Perhaps the 'interpretations' (translated into cold print) of these masterpieces, which now follow, will give the reader an inkling of the many potentialities of execution open to him and will lead him to experiment with the 'nine short notes' of which Mattheson speaks, instead of settling for an overall formula applied indiscriminately to all the wonders that Bach wrought in these five pages. There is a certain interdependence between bowing procedures and tempi and we cannot go far wrong if we consider a tempo of approximately ♩=82 as a fair average speed. Heifetz averages ♩=92. Dr Hans Bischoff in his edition of the clavier version of this Fugue suggests ♩=100, but this of course in keeping with the nature of the keyboard instrument. By the way, a look at this clavier version will show how important an element the descending and ascending chromatic line is in this Fugue. In this form it is notated throughout in crotchets: and is thus assured of the emphasis that violinists so often fail to give it. In its form as a violin Fugue, the chromatic line is played in quavers, but bow and vibrato stresses will give it its due and establish that balance between the

Ex. 12

and the somewhat *portato* descending or ascending chromatic line

Ex. 13

or

Ex. 14

that Bach so ideally realized.

But let me give some concrete examples of places where this need for variety—that I have been harping upon—makes itself most felt in this vast fugal edifice and let me give an idea how I have tried to come to grips with these problems.

About midway in the Fugue, where the theme comes in E minor, I adopt a smooth, suave, unarticulated bowing in piano for the four bars of the theme, which then changes in the next four bars to a more assertive, more articulated enunciation until it reaches the next goal—as it were. That is, the F major episode with its chromatic counter-subject, which in turn brings us to the eloquent

Ex. 15

that I am tempted to call one of the several 'natural divides' in the geography of this great work. The depth and weight of our G string I find of great help whenever I use it in places like the preceding one (instead of the D string in the more obvious first position) or in places like this, towards the end:

Ex. 16

In fact, many other bars too numerous to single out, such as:

Ex. 17

are enhanced in a very obvious way by the use of the G string in lieu of the D string.

The homophonic interludes in this Fugue are another point of great importance. If they are conceived by the player as what they are, commenting interludes between the polyphonic conflicts of the main body of the Fugue, and conceived as units of fifteen or so bars, played in a meaningful, unmechanical way, with a light, sometimes *floconneux* bow, thus avoiding the monotony that so easily creeps into so-called 'figuration' sequences of semiquavers (especially when played with identical barwise stresses!), then they will fulfil their role of oases in the prevailingly polyphonic texture. In my listening experience it is precisely in these interludes that performances get bogged down.

I have used the words 'commenting' and 'meaningful' of these homophonic interludes. The Bach scholar Arnold Schering reminds us that Bach —according to his biographer Forkel—likened polyphonic compositions to the concept of a group assembled for the purpose of earnest conversation, during which everyone voices his opinion, at first alone, then contradicting or confirming, or else remains silent in order to let the others have their say. These Fugues bring to mind not only this picture, but also monologues, solitary ruminations, dialogues. . . . Arnold Schering in his notes on the Brandenburg Concerto No. 6 does not hesitate to write that Bach here uses the upper register of the violas to such telling effect that 'it would not be difficult to consider these passages as sung by human voices and *furnish them with an appropriate* text'.

I hope that this short statement of my general approach to these Fugues will help to explain what I said earlier about the theme of the A minor Fugue. Not only is it wrong to omit the slurs in the two *legato* segments just because they are not in the manuscript; the slurs should be stressed, so as to give the necessary contrast to the prevailingly non-*legato* texture.

It goes without saying that this recommended stressing of the slurred

 applies equally to its mirrored form as in

Ex. 18

(It is interesting to note, by the way, that at this place the slurs are *not* missing in the manuscript.) The delicate bowing problem of doing justice to both the slurred ascending motif and the descending one faces us already in the fourth bar—and in corresponding places—where an unequal distribution of bow pressure becomes necessary, if we wish to emphasize the ascending motif. This problem becomes increasingly difficult to solve where the descending motif appears in chords as the 'rule' of the slurred motif is temporarily suspended, owing to the changed '*marcato*' context.

Ex. 19

The pedantically literal reading of a facsimile like that of the Bach Solo Sonatas can lead into absurdity.

When Bach in the G minor Violin Fugue notates:

Ex. 20

he undoubtedly means us to use some arpeggiated form of the sequence, and not play it as in the edition by J. Hellmesberger:

Ex. 21

From the early edition of F. David on all editors (except Hellmesberger) were agreed on this point.

F. David and Hubay:

Ex. 22

Flesch:

Ex. 23

Champeil:

Ex. 24

It is with reluctance that in this connection I mention the in many respects very painstaking and useful edition of the Sonatas and Partitas by the late K. Mostras (Edition Muzyka, Moscow 1965), who was one of the most respected pedagogues of the Soviet Union. But what other word than absurd is there for a notation of the above passage from the G minor Fugue that goes even further on the road of pedantic literalness than Hellmesberger did? Mostras, in fact, prints the whole passage of seven bars (see above) as it is found in Bach's manuscript, trying to combine *Texttreue* with (very doubtful) playability, by marking from the fourth bar on

Ex. 25

which after all can result only in an *approximation* of what Bach had in mind. In this passage Bach only put down the melodic and harmonic progression, leaving it to the player to *realize* the text by arpeggiating it.

The same kind of rigidity and unquestioning faithfulness to the *letter* of the text prompts Mostras to omit the obviously necessary and implied slurs, four and three bars from the end of the A minor Fugue, to notate the passages where trills are implied (as at the end of the Chaconne) without trills and to reproduce the sequence in the A minor Fugue in two alternative variants

110

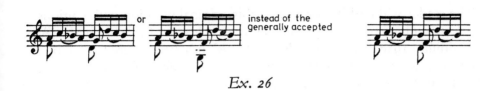

Ex. 26

One must respect the awe in which Mostras held the manuscript, yet he seems to have lost sight of the fact that the many marks of expression, the *cresc. poco a poco, allargandos, espressivos,* accents, *calandos* that he added already constitute a certain deviation from the original! As does every 'interpretation' of a text.

The authority of David D. Boyden's *The History of Violin Playing* should surely reassure any 'doubting Thomases' among my readers. It says (page 439): '. . . the word "*arpeggio*" is not always present in passages that quite probably were meant to be arpeggiated, Bach's first unaccompanied Sonata containing a good example'. (And the author specifically refers to bars 35–41 of the Fugue.)*

But as further reassurance to the student, let me give here an arpeggio passage in Corelli's Sonata Op. 5, No. 6, as printed with figured bass in the edition by 'J. Walsh, Servt to her Majesty at ye Harp & Hoboy in Katherine street in ye Strand & J.Harl at ye Viol & Flute in Cornhill nere ye Royal Exchange'.

Ex. 27

---

* In the Chaconne Bach did mark the instruction 'Arpeggio' after giving a model of it.

The reader will find by comparing this original notation with editions like Schott's (Jensen) dating back to the 1880s or Carl Fischer's (Albert Spalding, 1930) that Corelli's '*Arpeggio*' has been disregarded by later editors, just as Bach's *implied arpeggio* in the G minor Fugue has been, and that the *arpeggios* have been notated as chords! In the formerly much played First Sonata (D major) of Corelli's Op. 5, we again find eleven and a half bars marked *Arpeggio*, but this indication has been respected, that is, realized by later editors like Jensen and Hellmesberger.

The bridge leading into the A minor Fugue is still more of a puzzle than these *arpeggio* passages on account of the ⌇⌇⌇⌇⌇ sign Bach put on top of both of the two crotchets, adding the 'tr' sign only to the second of these.

The following tabulation will show in how many different ways this has been (and is being) interpreted. Heifetz, for instance, brings off the feat (in his recording) of executing a trill in sixths with a 1.2 and 3.4 fingering as he assumes that the ⌇⌇⌇⌇ sign implies this double trill. None of the editors to my knowledge makes this demand on the performer.

Ex. 28

Probably the most noticeable of the controversial divergencies in readings are in the opening and closing bars of the Chaconne, simply because this work, of all the six sonatas and partitas, is the most often played. I say 'noticeable' advisedly, because it is at the beginning and end of such a work that any deviation from the norm to which listeners have become accustomed stands out most clearly.

There are two factions (if one may use such a word). The one adheres to the letter of the manuscript and plays the last quaver of the first and second bars not as a chord but as a single note, and concludes the work without a trill in the penultimate bar. Joachim, Busch, E. Polo, Anzelotti, Mostras, Enesco and Champeil print or play it thus, although only Enesco, Mostras and Champeil entirely omit the trill in the penultimate bar.

The other, more numerous group uses the traditional version, with the last quaver in the first two bars as a chord and ending on the cadential trill. To this group belong David, Hellmesberger, Capet, Flesch, Hubay, Heifetz, Maglioni, Jan Hambourg and myself. Busoni's famous transcription for piano and all quartet and orchestral transcriptions adhere to this interpretation.

In detail, the readings are as follows:
The manuscript has:

Ex. 29

Paul Lemaitre (1951), Günter Hauswald (1959) and K. Mostras (Moscow, 1965) follow this text.

Joachim and several of his followers print:

Ex. 30

Flesch has:

Ex. 31

and is very explicit about the loss of grandeur and power that the previous reading entails.

Hubay prints:

Ex. 32

and the majority of editions and performers (for instance Jan Hambourg, Oxford University Press, 1935, and Francescatti) follow Flesch and Hubay.

Champeil, maintaining, with Quantz and other authorities on the eighteenth century, that a quaver coming after a dotted crotchet should be executed as a semiquaver coming after a double-dotted crotchet, proposes:

Ex. 33

On this thesis, the quaver (played as a semiquaver) could hardly be played as a chord; and on his thesis, incidentally, the distortion of the dotted first

variation ♪♩.♪♩.♪♩♪♩ into a triplet rhythm ♩♩♪♪♩♪ ♪—alas,

still so common, in spite of Flesch's warning in his full-length discussion of the Chaconne in the second volume of his *Art of Violin Playing*—becomes doubly regrettable.

David D. Boyden in his *History of Violin Playing* does go so far as to say that the chordless last quaver in the first bar of the Chaconne 'may indeed have been the way intended by Bach'. In this sentence I prefer to stress the word 'may'.

Sol Babitz, who has given much thought to these questions, thinks that the opening of the Chaconne should be played as the manuscript has it, but somewhat in the dancelike manner suggested by Champeil. As a sample of the 'mild 3:2 inequality' with which a Sarabande (also in ¾ time, and somewhat similar to a Chaconne) should be played, he gives me the following 'realization' of the first part of the B minor Sarabande as he imagines it to have been played at the time:

Ex. 34

If I now quote three transcriptions, two for string quartet and Busoni's famous one for piano, it is not with the object of discussing the merits and demerits of transcriptions as such, but only for the light which they can throw upon the validity of a tradition and the effect of fashion on the reading of a text.

Transcription by Luigi Schinina (Ed. Curci):

Ex. 35

Busoni transcription (Breitkopf & Härtel):

Ex. 36

A. M. Herz (Simrock):

Ex. 37

The endings show these differences: trill and endings on double D's. David, Hellmesberger, Flesch, Capet:

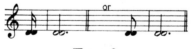

Ex. 38

Maglioni:

Ex. 39

Hubay:

Ex. 40

Heifetz ends on a legato slide from E to D.
Francescatti plays:

Ex. 41

Busch plays and prints:

Ex. 42

Champeil, true to the principle of 'double-dotting', notates:

Ex. 43

Jan Hambourg has:

Ex. 44

and K. Mostras:

Ex. 45

Polo:

Ex. 46

Anzoletti:

Ex. 47

An article by Raymond Leppard in the magazine *Performing Right* (April 1968) is relevant here. Speaking of 'an extraordinarily simple and imprecise notation' which existed when, at the beginning of the seventeenth century, music turned from 'polyphonic to continuo-based' practice, he suggests that 'the very inexactness was welcomed as a liberating creative factor to which many others besides the composer were called upon to contribute'. He concedes that to a mind conditioned to the idea of a sacrosanct *Urtext* much of what he says will be hard to accept; and he draws a distinction between *Urtext*-minded and *Urgeist*-minded which is worth thinking about.

How fluid and ephemeral all these outlooks and interpretations are, compared with the eternal quality of the music itself! If the purist today goes—as I think—too far in playing the last quaver of the first and second bars without the chord, Joseph Hellmesberger, in his edition (Peters) which was the most used version for several decades about the turn of the century, certainly went to the other extreme when he advocated playing the entire theme with *downbow chords*. This false 'monumentality' would raise a smile today; yet at the time, probably thousands of violinists played it thus and tens of thousands of listeners accepted it at its face value.

Where we today favour the cadence

Ex. 48

in the Sonata in G minor, first movement, and

Ex. 49

in the Sonata in A minor, first movement, the majority of players (Joachim among them) used the versions

Ex. 50

and

Ex. 51

seventy or eighty years ago.

And at the end of the first movement of the G minor Solo Sonata, where Bach wrote:

Ex. 52

Joachim wrote

Ex. 53

in his edition of the sonatas but he played

Ex. 54

adding a chord, D and A, to the cadential F.

And in the Chaconne, the cadence leading to the middle part of the triptych (the section in D major) is played and notated in two different ways: with the *appoggiatura* (B natural) by Joachim, Hubay and others; without it by Flesch, Capet, Hellmesberger, Champeil and others. Such examples could be multiplied by the dozen. Agreement on even such simple, basic questions seems impossible.

And what of the tempo of the Chaconne? We can use, as a safe guide, Carl Flesch's tentative metronome marking ♩ = 60, combined with Busoni's *Andante maestoso ma non troppo lento*; but the real problem is not the right tempo for the exposition of the theme, but how to maintain a continuous line during our journey through the 'worlds' that Bach created out of the theme. For they are truly worlds apart in content, *Stimmung*, lyricism, monumentality. Only the player who makes the hearer conscious of the basic syncopated tread (the origin of all that grows out of it) will succeed in welding together all these visions into a whole. It is, of course, impossible to maintain a rigid tempo in the neighbourhood of $\sharp = 60$ throughout, but it stands to reason that tempo fluctuations (and I have tested metronomically fluctuations ranging from $\sharp = 56$ to $\sharp = 84$) cannot result in a unified view of this towering masterpiece.

I take no little pride in having steadfastly refused offers from publishers to add still another annotated edition (based on the photostat of the manuscript, of course!) to the bewildering number already available. Judging by my own experience, remembering the continuous changes that my own playing of these great works underwent in the course of years, I feel the futility of such an undertaking; and I prefer to give in these pages a glimpse of the contradictions that face anyone who attempts to lay down the law.

The so-called 'Joachim edition' was published in 1909, two years after the great Bach interpreter's death, and though one cannot doubt the painstaking faithfulness of his collaborator, Andreas Moser, to Joachim's instructions and advice (and to his fingerings and bowings, which must have been placed at Moser's disposal), it is easy to imagine that editorial work undertaken so late in life, when the problems encountered had no longer the burning actuality they had for the pioneering performer that Joachim must have been in his fifties, cannot be considered a valid legacy.

It comes down to this: every one of us must work out his own salvation, remembering what Alfred Frankenstein once wrote (precisely *à propos* of a recording of the set of Bach Sonatas) '. . . everything that comes down from the past, including such apparently changeless things as pyramids and paintings, must always be interpreted afresh in the light of each generation's temperament, scholarship and creative preoccupation.'

Even such dedicated Bach enthusiasts as Casals and Adolf Busch could not see eye to eye on questions of Bach interpretations;* and it is a significant fact that Casals, to whom their renaissance is due, never published an edition of the Cello Suites. (This, of course, will not prevent a proliferation of 'authentic Casals editions' in the 1980s and 1990s by pupils and pupils of pupils . . .) How then can one hope to find the way out of this labyrinth of conflicting readings except by individual soul-searching followed by courageous decisions?

---

* *The biographer of Adolf Busch tells of the twenty-one-year-old violinist's meeting with Casals in 1912 and of the outspoken discussion (not to say dispute) between the young man and the most celebrated of cellists and Bach interpreters, then thirty-six years old, about divergences in their outlook.*

CHAPTER 19

FOLLOWS THE CHANGES IN OUR
appreciation of the unaccompanied sonatas and partitas
over the last hundred years

To UNDERSTAND the reason for this lack of agreement in our outlook today (in the 1960s) on essential questions of Bach interpretation we should take a look at the 'status' which the unaccompanied sonatas and partitas had, say, a hundred years ago. They were not considered—as they are today—indispensable pillars of our musical and violinistic equipment; they were seldom played; there was something apologetic in the minds of those *virtuosi* who did play parts of them (sometimes with piano accompaniment).

The first editions were those published by Simrock in 1802, with those by Ferdinand David (1810–73) and Joseph Hellmesberger (1828–93) following presumably in the 1860s or 70s.

Robert Schumann and Felix Mendelssohn, with the laudable object of rescuing them from their position of step-children, as it were, among the works of Bach, and of making them available (or, one might say, palatable) to a wider public, thought it necessary to provide the works, which so perfectly carry out their author's intention in their original form, with pianoforte accompaniments.

There is no need today for me to waste words pointing out that in this they acted on a misconception of the essential nature of these works. Such a misunderstanding on the part of these two great masters is largely attributable to the spirit of their time, and we need not pursue the matter further here.

As a boy, I myself was guilty of performing single movements of these works in public with Schumann's pianoforte accompaniments. But this came to an end when Busoni explained the impropriety of such an abuse—talking to me like a father at a concert we gave together somewhere in the

Midlands in 1908 or 1909—and opened my eyes about this, as he did on so many other musical matters.

It was not till our century that the rash of editions and interpretations started. Interpretations that range all the way from a fluting, *piano, sur la touche* statement of fugue subjects to the heavy-fisted approach with a multitude of accent signs and G string over-emphasis. These were the inevitable growing pains in the performing style of these works before they achieved the status they have today, when no youngster can think of entering a competition without meeting the challenge of a Bach Solo Sonata. (It is well to remember that the proliferation of competitions started with the 1937 Brussels Ysaÿe—later Queen Elizabeth—competition; and to remember that the repertoire requirements of these competitions undoubtedly have an influence on the class-room schedule these days, with the result that what used to be a noteworthy feat a decade or so ago became a routine accomplishment a few years later.)

When the Montreal Competition of 1966, for instance, chose as *morceau imposé*, Bartók's Solo Sonata (first movement) it meant that some three dozen young violinists and their teachers (who may, for all we know, execrate this wonderful piece and who grope about its 'dark secrets' with something like desperation) sweated over it for months. Thus mastery of such a work becomes a routine requirement in the next decades (as Ravel's 'Scarbo' and Beethoven's Op. 106 Sonata have become for pianists). The Bach Solo Sonatas had no such short-cuts to general acceptance and performance standards. There were no recordings of a complete four-movement Sonata before 1932. My recordings of the A minor and the G minor were the first Bach Sonatas ever to be released.

It is characteristic of the spirit which prevailed in the first decade of this century that in my early years J never heard a public performance of the two Sonatas in C major and A minor, although in those years I heard Kreisler, Marteau, Kubelik, Elman, Thibaud, Ysaÿe, Sarasate, Petschnikoff, and others. At that time it was mostly only single movements that were played in public, like the Prelude of the E major Partita, dashed off as fast as possible, and above all the Chaconne, which has earned for itself a place apart.

The change came with Adolf Busch, Huberman, and a handful of others (Busch's admirable edition of the Sonatas dates from 1919). The way the famous Prelude of the E major Partita used to be treated in the Sarasate–Kubelik period, as a technical showpiece to be rattled off at the highest possible speed, was typical of the complete misunderstanding at the time of the essential nature of the Bach Sonatas. Willi Burmester, whom I often used to hear around 1905 or so, played as encores single movements (such as the E major Prelude) with his own pianoforte accompaniments. To think that this was the same E major Prelude which Bach himself valued so highly that he used it as the introduction to his Cantata '*Wir danken dir, Gott, wir danken dir*', and scored it for organ, three trumpets, two oboes, and percussion and strings. The title of this marvellous elaboration is Sinfonia from Cantata No. 29.

Incidentally, Bach also used the fugues from the G minor and the C major Sonatas for Cantatas—the G minor Fugue for '*Ich hatte viel Bekümmernis*', and the C major for '*Komm, heiliger Geist, Herre Gott*'. It is said that books have a destiny of their own; the same can be said of musical compositions.

In these few pages devoted to the Bach Solo Sonatas and Partitas, I have limited myself to tabulating different 'readings', giving in just a very few cases a glimpse into my workshop (the A minor Fugue is a case in point). To attempt anything more would have been a futile undertaking. Thus I do not discuss anything pertaining to the three Partitas except the Allemande and the opening and closing bars of the Chaconne from the Partita in D minor. An analysis of the colossal edifice of the Chaconne, in which, as Schweitzer says, Bach has conjured up 'a whole world' out of a single short theme, would lead too far.

The problem for player and listener alike is to be conscious of the essential unity of the work in its bewildering diversity, to realize its triptych-like character (with the first fifteen variations in minor, the next nine in major, and the remainder in minor once again); also to be conscious (and make the listener conscious) of the way variation generates variation, thus creating clusters of variations. Paul Henry Lang says about these six works: 'Fantastic preludes, completely developed fugues, and cyclopean variations alternate in these Sonatas with graceful dances. Creative imagination fixes in them its absolute triumph over all restrictions and limitations imposed upon it by form, material and medium of expression.'

It is curious that Bach's role as an innovator, violinistically speaking, has not been sufficiently stressed by commentators. The device of an 'apparent' organ point which he uses in the D major section of the Chaconne, where he hammers the reiterated A's (successively in three octaves) into our consciousness is an extraordinary stroke of instrumental ingenuity, to mention but one instance.

All the more reason for violinists to look out for works that can serve as stepping stones towards this supreme challenge, such as the Sonatas by Biber (1644–1704) and Pisendel (1687–1755). A glance at Pisendel's Solo Sonata in A minor—Pisendel was about thirty years of age when Bach started writing his Sonatas—will bear out my supposition that Bach was familiar with the great Dresden Concertmaster's playing style and with the Solo Sonatas. Familiarity with such stepping stones to what Bach ultimately achieved can only enhance our admiration of his fulfilment.

We of the twentieth century can pride ourselves on having advanced the cause of these great works appreciably. (Just as the rediscovery of that other treasure-trove, the Mozart Piano Concertos, can be a source of pride to those pianists of the last thirty-five or forty years who have devoted themselves to them.) For the resistance to works like the Bach Solo Sonatas in the nineteenth century is something difficult to visualize today. Even a perceptive critic like George Bernard Shaw could write about Joachim's performance of the C major Fugue (28 February 1890):

> He played Bach's Sonata in C at the Bach Choir Concert at St James's Hall on Tuesday. The second movement of that work is a fugue three or four hundred bars long. Of course you cannot really play fugue in three continuous parts on the violin; but by dint of double stopping and dodging from one part to another, you can evoke a hideous ghost of a fugue that will pass current if guaranteed by Bach and Joachim. That was what happened on Tuesday. Joachim scraped away frantically, making a sound after which an attempt to grate a nutmeg effectively on a boot sole would have been as the strain of an Aeolian harp. The notes which were musical enough to have any discernible pitch at all were mostly out of tune. It was horrible—damnable! Had he been an unknown player, introducing an unknown composer, he would not have escaped with his life. Yet we all—I no less than the others—were interested and enthusiastic. We applauded like anything; and he bowed to us with unimpaired gravity. The dignified artistic career of Joachim and the grandeur of Bach's reputation had so hypnotized us that we took an abominable noise for the music of the spheres.

Even though much in these works still eludes us (in spite of our advances in technique and the familiarity of the listener with this idiom), we can safely say that we have come a long way from G. B. Shaw's 'abominable noise'. . . .

CHAPTER 20

SOME BACH MISPRINTS;
and some others

As a kind of footnote to my Bach chapters I set down here a few of the misprints and omissions in which most editions of the Sonatas and Partitas abound:

Nineteen bars before the end of the G minor Fugue the lower F in

Ex. 1

is missing in all editions except the Oxford University Press one. Flesch prints the F in the lower (MS.) line, but not in the upper one.

In the Siciliana of the G minor Sonata practically all editors give C instead of D

Ex. 2

Only Busch gives the D, and he merely as an alternative in a footnote.

In the G minor Fugue, Joachim, Busch and Maglioni print the right text:

Ex. 3

while Hubay, Hellmesberger and F. David make this unwarranted change:

Ex. 4

Later in this Fugue the Manuscript has:

Ex. 5

while Ernst Kurth, Champeil prints:

Ex. 6

I particularly wish to draw attention to the—to my mind—false interpretation of this passage in the Chaconne:

Ex. 7

which has come to be generally printed and played in this fashion:

Ex. 8

The fact that Bach notated the bass throughout with a unison (double) D, indicates his wish that the passage should have a four-part texture. This can only be realized if it is played in this way:

Ex. 9

Fortunately one no longer hears the F. David and Capet edition's misprint in the Chaconne:

Ex. 10

instead of the correct:

Ex. 11

Almost all editions of the Chaconne (with the praiseworthy exception of Busch, Capet, Hellmesberger) print E instead of D (soon after the return to the minor).

Ex. 12

To hear this E sometimes twenty times in a row at some competition where the Chaconne is obligatory, is an ordeal indeed!

In the eleventh bar before the end of the Prelude in E several editors still persist in printing G sharp instead of A:

Ex. 13

This passage in the 'Double' of the Sarabande (B minor Partita) can be found in different readings in some editions: the MS. has

Ex. 14

and not:

Ex. 15

In the Sarabande of the B minor Partita all editions that I have seen choose to ignore the manuscript's notation of

Ex. 16

and they print instead:

Ex. 17

The edition by Busch is the only exception. In his earlier 1919 edition the right text is given only as an alternative, in a footnote, but in his 1931 edition he incorporates it in the text.

It is incomprehensible to me why Flesch gave, as an alternative in the thirteenth bar of the Grave of the A minor Sonata, C sharp (in brackets, it's true!), when the descending bass line unequivocally demands a C natural. We see what toughness misprints show in their capacity for survival, in spite of manuscripts and *Urtexts*. . . .

*

How unsuspectingly we keep on playing misprints and passing these on to our pupils was brought home to me when I was asked to compile a list of some of these for the venerable *Neue Zeitschrift für Musik*, founded by Robert Schumann in 1834 and still in full activity. Such a list seems particularly timely today, when publishers like Dr G. Henle, of the Henle *Urtext* Edition, Duisburg, try to remedy the publishing malpractices I have mentioned in chapter 14 (in connection with the Schumann A minor Sonata) by utilizing every available resource of research and scholarship in order to present us with exemplary texts. Here then are some examples:

Beethoven 'Kreutzer' Sonata Op. 47. First movement, bar 95: according to the Henle edition, based on the *Stichvorlage*, it should be:

Ex. 18

not F double sharp as in the Joachim–Peters edition. The same goes, of course, for the parallel bar 416, where the turn has to be on B natural.

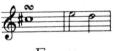

Ex. 19

Beethoven Sonata Op. 96. First movement bar 127 (piano part):

Ex. 20

The first note should be F natural, not F sharp. Bar 158—the violin should play A flat (fifth note of bar), not A natural as in Joachim–Peters and some other editions.

Ex. 21

In the fourth movement, bar 218, the piano part has

Ex. 22

that is, G natural in the autograph, original edition and early printings; this will come to most of us as something of a shock, used as we are to the G sharp in later editions!

Beethoven Violin Concerto. First movement (G minor theme): This should be:

Ex. 23

(a crotchet rest and triplet).

Beethoven Sonata Op. 30 No. 1. Last movement (Variation I): Joachim has

Ex. 24

instead of

Ex. 25

Mozart Sonata K. 378, second movement, bar 20: the Schnabel–Flesch edition has:

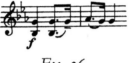

instead of:

Ex. 26

The comparatively recent edition of the Paganini Caprices based on the manuscript (Suvini–Zerboni, Milan) has rectified a misinterpretation in the recapitulation of Caprice XVII.
It should read:

Ex. 27

and not:

Ex. 28

Schnabel and I, while rehearsing the last movement of the Brahms Sonata in G major, Op. 78, suddenly realized that—in common with practically all other sonata teams—we had played C naturals in the last quaver of this bar:

Ex. 29

instead of the beautifully dissonant C sharps!

But perhaps the most humiliating discovery that the Henle edition has brought to light is the opening of the last movement of the Mozart Sonata K. 454, that has been printed, played, recorded (by myself among others) with the *sfp* on the G and F instead of as in the autograph:

Ex. 30

These samplings of misprints, misunderstandings and misinterpretations are not only offered as a list of errata, to be pencilled into one's own copies of these works. They are also meant to demonstrate how naïve it is to put blind faith in any one edition or even in an *Urtext* based on a photostat of a manuscript. And they will—I hope—counteract the impression I may have given that I—in common with the many learned guardians of *Urtexts*—look upon the use of a faultless score as something like a guarantee of a stylish performance. That nothing could be further from my thought has—I trust—been apparent all along.

Anyone who has handled the Mozart *Ten Celebrated Quartets* in Dr Alfred Einstein's magnificent edition (Novello, 1954) and looked at some of his 'Critical Reports' (resulting from his comparison of the autographs, the original edition and the 'Collected Works' version) will have been cured of any tendency he may have had to consider any *Urtext* edition whatsoever as sacrosanct. And anyone who has studied the problem of realizing in performance what was meant by the composer at the time when he wrote a *staccato* or dash and dot, or wedge-shaped, or tear-drop-shaped sign, will be wary of using the word *Texttreue*, as applied to performances today of masterpieces of the past.

It is sobering indeed to dip into David D. Boyden's chapter on 'Culmination of early Violin Playing, 1700–1761' in his monumental *History of Violin Playing* and read about the confusions in the performance markings of some of these manuscripts.

The humility of such scholars in comparison with the cocksureness—in questions of performance—of some of our critics and university lecturers is very revealing.

CHAPTER 21

QUESTIONS WHETHER THE UNCERTAINTIES
caused by the disagreement of editors are not sometimes
responsible for the neglect of certain compositions. Liberties
taken by editors with Tartini, Corelli, and Handel are discussed

How many of the works of the great Italians do we hear on the programmes of most of our violinists? No more, it seems to me, than the 'Devil's Trill' Sonata with Kreisler's elaborate *cadenza, La Follía* of Corelli (No. XII of his Op. 5) in a more or less spurious edition, mostly the version by Léonard, the short Vivaldi A major Sonata, in the reworking either by David, Respighi or Adolf Busch, and Tommaso Vitali's Chaconne.

Informed musicological opinion now attributes this Chaconne to an anonymous composer of the late eighteenth century and neither to Giovanni Battista Vitali nor to his son Tommaso Antonio. The younger Tommaso Vitali lived between 1665 and 1706 and his other works do not suggest that he is the author of this set of variations, whose modulations through remote keys caused M. Rinaldi to voice his doubts of their authenticity in the *Rassegna Musicale* in 1954. It has, however, conquered through its undeniable beauty, theatrical pathos and effectiveness, whoever composed it. (I used to play it with organ and string orchestra in Respighi's transcription and I remember hearing Ysaÿe play it with an accompaniment of organ *and* piano!)

The much less often performed but lovely Tartini Sonata in G minor (*Didone Abbandonata*) about completes this list of the half-dozen works that *virtuosi* still consider 'safe' material with the increasingly heterogeneous public of subscription concerts in the middle of the twentieth century.

The Prelude and Allegro 'in the style of Pugnani' by Kreisler, and his arrangement of three out of the fifty variations of Tartini's *L'Arte dell' Arco* should perhaps be mentioned too, as numbers that the public accepts as Italian baroque.

Lesser known and more authentically edited baroque works are being played at gatherings for baroque *aficionados*, and many chamber orchestras on their tours make these known to the general public, but this does not invalidate what I say about the programme policy of some of our star violinists. And I am not, of course, speaking here about the début recital by ambitious younger players who wish to attract the attention of the press by more adventurous fare. But when it comes to concerts by stars, who cater for the less knowledgeable general public, we shall probably find one of the above-mentioned Italian pieces on the list—with the Bach Chaconne, the 'Spring' Sonata, and some Sarasate, Paganini and *moto perpetuo* items, and perhaps some Szymanowski or Saint-Saëns in the last (interchangeable) group.

In these circumstances it is not surprising that the concert-goer who not only 'knows what he likes' but 'likes what he knows' continues to live in the fond illusion that *La Follías*, doctored-up Vitali Chaconnes and Pugnani Allegros are the sum total of what Italy has brought to violin literature.

Why is it that Corelli's Sonatas, Op. 5, which were a landmark in their time and were reprinted—that is, pirated—an unprecedented number of times, have practically disappeared from our star violinists' programmes, along with the dozens of Tartini Sonatas that have been reprinted in the last sixty years? I have no doubt that our neglect is in large part due to the inconsistency and inadequacy of the versions available, whose editors, most of them viewing these works through late nineteenth-century spectacles, give no clue to the approximately correct style of presentation.

It is enlightening, for instance, to see how Corelli's essential embellishments are being gradually eliminated. Compare Kreisler's version of the slow movement of the First Sonata of Op. 5, in D major, which dispenses with embellishments altogether, with the original edition, which prints so many. Jensen (*c.* 1880) retains a few of these; Hellmesberger and Kreisler use only the unadorned melody. In the Sixth Sonata, in A major, Jensen prints

Ex. 1

137

This is reduced by Albert Spalding in 1930 to:

Ex. 2

One wonders whether in the 1980s this will be reduced to:

Ex. 3

In the J. Walsh edition of 1713, the bar reads thus:

Ex. 4

Even Tartini's important and perennially popular 'Devil's Trill' Sonata has not escaped editorial distortion. Of all the editions at present available only two have preserved the original double-stopped statement of the lovely Siciliana-like first movement; and as these two (Hubay's (Bosworth) and T. Nachez's (Schott)) are less used than those of Joachim, Kreisler, Edition Peters and others, we take for granted the suppression of the necessary and enhancing accompanying lower voice.

Jean Baptiste Cartier (1765–1841) was the first to publish this daring masterpiece in 1798 from the manuscript given or lent to him by Baillot. It was included in his volume *L'Art du Violon* which was an epoch-making anthology in its time and is of such historical interest even today that, according to rumour, it is due for a presumably facsimile-reprint, within a year or two, by an American reprint firm. (The beautifully engraved title-page shows six portrait-medallions: those of G. Tartini, A. Corelli, P. Gaviniès, M. Leclair, L. Mozart and G. Stamitz.)

The edition that (presumably) followed this first and more or less faithful one by J. B. Cartier, was that by the illustrious Henri Vieuxtemps (1820–81), published by Jean André in Offenbach-sur-Main. It already suppressed the original double-stopping version and has an accompaniment for 'either Piano or String Quartet'. The last Allegro is changed by Vieuxtemps in such a way that it joins on to his own Cadenza, which in turn culminates in a very questionable grandiloquent version in octaves and chords of the original Largo, whose last bars Vieuxtemps changed to:

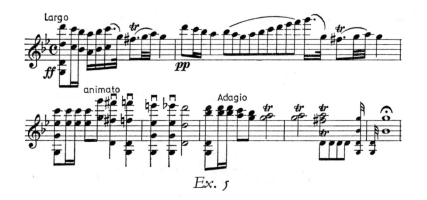

Ex. 5

No wonder that those who came after Vieuxtemps felt free to commit still further and more reprehensible distortions in the name of 'liberty' of inter-pretation.

Here is a tabulation starting with J. B. Cartier's text and showing the subsequent vicissitudes of this text.

Ex. 6

A handwritten copy in Brussels Royal Conservatoire Library, probably late eighteenth century:

Ex. 7

Breitkopf & Härtel, Leipzig, probably the end of the eighteenth century:

Ex. 8

Henri Vieuxtemps (1820–81), reprinted in Moscow in 1933 with fingerings by G. Dulow:

Ex. 9

This version by Fritz Kreisler (1875–1962) was published in 1905. Joachim's 1905 edition and the Peters edition (Friedrich Hermann) are almost identical with Kreisler's in the opening movement.

Ex. 10

The 1914 version by T. Nachez (1859–1930). Hubay's version was very similar to the Cartier text.

Ex. 11

The *Hohe Schule des Violinspiels* of Ferdinand David (1810–73) would yield similar instructive examples of textual and stylistic distortions, if compared with the manuscripts and first editions of the works it contains.

Having written at length of one of Tartini's many dozens of Sonatas, I feel the reader should be reminded that beside the Sonatas, there exist some 250 Tartini Concertos, of which only one, the D minor (which I recorded twice and edited for Carl Fischer in New York), can be called familiar.

Of the Sonatas, I only played and recorded *one* (beside the 'Devil's Trill'): the one in G major in H. Léonard's edition (Schott Frères Brussels). The beautiful one in A minor in this same series used to be played by Enesco. It is with a sense of contrition that I put down these words: 'I only played one'; and I know that I have been defeated by the difficulty of deciding which of the available editions to follow. I am afraid the answer is: we cannot follow blindly *any* of these. All we can do is to collate, that is, compare different versions, go in for some soul-searching and for some—admittedly amateurish—musicological research among photostats of manuscripts or first editions.

Some of the problems that face the conscientious, style-conscious student have already been shown on the preceding pages; other examples will follow. It is up to the reader to draw conclusions.

We have always known that editorial distortions of the kind I have described in this chapter did exist. But it was quite a shock to me—and will no doubt also shock my readers—to find out, recently, that the last movement of the D major Sonata of Handel had been amputated by exactly eighteen bars (out of seventy-two!) in all currently available editions. I, like all contemporary violinists, had played and recorded it in this truncated version, and it is only now that the 1955 edition (Max Schneider) of the G. F. Handel Gesellschaft (Deutscher Verlag für Musik, Leipzig) showed me these excisions by the conventional signs 'vi–de'.

What is astonishing is that even such scholarly editors as Chrysander in the old *Handelgesellschaft* and Gevaert (approximately 1885, Breitkopf) made no mention of these cuts, even in a footnote. A glance at the unexpurgated movement is sufficient to show the logic of the excised bars which repeat the semiquaver passage of the violin most effectively in the bass of the keyboard instrument.*

* *What has been said in the preceding pages applies equally to masterpieces of the French School, for instance to the fine (and nowadays neglected) Sonata in D major by Jean-Marie Leclair (1697–1764) which contains the Sarabande and Tambourin, formerly a popular number on Sarasate's and other great virtuosos' programmes.*

CHAPTER 22

EXAMINES SOME MORE TEXTUAL
problems—and Beethoven's changes of mind in the Violin
Concerto

THERE IS another salutary shock in store for the violinist in Alan Tyson's extraordinarily enlightening enquiry into some of the puzzles connected with the Beethoven Violin Concerto (*Music and Letters*, April 1962, 'The Text of Beethoven's Op. 61'). In this he shows that 'the corruptions in the Violin Concerto are certainly as old as the first edition of 1808' and he calls the autograph, which is now in the National Bibliothek, Vienna, 'a confusing document', one that has several alternative lines for the solo violin, in short, a document in which he sees 'signs of uncertainty as well as of haste'. He reminds us of the circumstances of that historic *première* when Clement played this Concerto of all Concertos (as Joachim called it) practically '*prima vista*', having received it scarcely two days before the concert, and he adds that this haste accounts 'for the impression that Beethoven was partly still composing the work while he was writing it out'.

Mr Tyson gives us answers to several questions, such as the cello response to the bassoon in bars 525–6 of the first movement; he gives us 'The Case of the Missing Bar' (as bar 217 in the Rondo): how it first got left out, and how it was reinstated in our times; and he tells how the 'two witty *pizzicato* notes in bar 218' were apparently an afterthought of the composer and how an *espressivo* had been misread by the engraver as *sempre fsimo*, that is, *sempre fortissimo*—the first 's' of the double 's' being written long and thus hardly distinguishable from an 'f'. (When I first studied the Beethoven Concerto with Hubay, some sixty-five years ago, he had not yet published his own edition and I used the old Peters version by Wilhelmj (Plate No. 6718) in which bar 217 was missing—and was not missed at the time, at least, not by us. . . .) What I consider most thought-provoking in Mr Tyson's essay, from the point of view of students of today, is that it makes it clear that Beethoven 'was not particularly concerned to make up his mind about a detail or to resolve an inconsistency' and that 'in these cases we have to make up his mind for him, keeping a sense of proportion, but not relying too slavishly on what we find in the first edition'.

A courageous statement indeed, and one which corroborates the attitude of George Szell, a musician of proverbial integrity, who, debating the inconsistency of a composer's markings with his concertmaster, recently said: 'The composers want us to be imaginative in the direction of their thinking—not just robots who execute an order.'

In the face of some critics' arrogant claims to know exactly what the composer meant when he penned this or that slur or dot 'with differing degrees of impatience' (as Alan Tyson writes) it is instructive to remember how little the creative mind resembles these '*Urtext*- critics' in their rigid laying down of the law. The student should remember not only how often composers have been quite willing to undertake transcriptions which— they were perfectly aware of this!—could not possibly be equivalent to the original (for instance, the César Franck Sonata transcribed for cello, Stravinsky's '*Histoire d'un Soldat*' Suite for Piano, Violin and Clarinet, Alban Berg's *Kammerkonzert* transcribed for these same instruments). They should also consider the liberality and elasticity of a Bartók who offers alternative endings to the performer in both the 1938 Violin Concerto and the 1928 First Violin Rhapsody (besides authorizing the performance of either the 'Lassu' or the 'Friss' as a separate piece!). Composers *do* have second thoughts, and their mind is less rigidly 'made up' than we assume. In the François Lang collection of music (at Royaumont near Paris) I have counted some two dozen changes in Debussy's hand in the first edition of *L'Après-midi d'un Faune*. . . .

How right Alan Tyson is when he refers to the Concerto as 'a work which has had so unfortunate a textual history as Beethoven's Op. 61'! I was reminded of much in the preceding pages when recently I was taken to task (in print) by a student of musicology for 'changing [in my edition] the bowing and *staccato* markings of Beethoven in the first eight bars of the last movement' and thereby 'heavy-handedly' destroying 'the subtlety by normalizing all the delicate variants'.

The facts of this 'destruction' can be summarized as follows: there are two 'schools of thought' in this question: the one favours a slur between the A and the D of the theme (G string):

Ex. 1

the other detaches (on one bow) the A from the D.

Ex. 2

The slurred approach necessitates either the fingering suggested by Wilhelmj in the already mentioned undependable old Peters edition:

Ex. 3

with the (to our ears) unwelcome slide, or the Joachim and Sauret fingering

Ex. 4

which involves any player who is less than a superb technician in a bumpy and perilous jump from first position to fifth (between D and F sharp) and back.

Carl Flesch in his 1915 and 1927 (Peters) edition rallied to the bowing that detaches the A from the D and allows the player to negotiate the change from first to fourth position during the pause with a maximum of rhythmic incisiveness and safety, and moreover in complete agreement with all the subsequent statements of the theme by the orchestra. He wrote, in fact: 'In most editions the dot is missing on the first two bars of the main theme. The editor prefers the given reading conformable with the original manuscript.'

In fact, the manuscript can be made to support either reading. It has an unmistakable slur between the A and the D (though possibly in a different ink from that of the notes), and above this D there is a mark which has been read as the fingering '1' (it seems unlikely that Beethoven would have written this in himself, and, if it is a fingering, it is more probably some violinist's practical suggestion); but it may equally well be a somewhat elongated dot.

Every one of the performances or recordings of Op. 61 I have heard (and this means a good many) has followed the reasoning of Flesch. (Hubay, who had studied with Joachim, used the same bowing in his edition of about 1910 and so does Francescatti in his recent publication.)

This consensus on the part of those who perform and record the Concerto surely does mean something, but this need not detain us here. What does concern us is rather the fact that *Texttreue*, far from enabling us to realize the 'subtlety' (which I was accused of destroying) could lead to unwanted, involuntary accents on the F sharp (if the Joachim jump from first to fourth position is used) or to an unstylish slide (if the Wilhelmj and Sauret fingering is followed).

It is precisely these F sharps that are the danger points and that would invalidate the all-important *tenutos* on the A's and lead to what we all want to avoid: a jog-trot, over-accented delivery something like this:

Ex. 5

Carl Czerny (1791–1857), Beethoven's pupil between 1801 and 1803, in his writings about his master gives the theme of the Rondo in its version for Piano and Orchestra, with this orthography:

Ex. 6

with the dots *below* the slur. (By the way he calls it 'vielleicht sein grösstes und schönstes Konzert'.)

Dots above the slurs, dots below the slurs, phrasings predicated by the nature of the piano, or congenial to the bowed instrument that can realize a dotted note in a variety of manners: at the tip of the bow (downbow), at the nut or middle (upbow) in different degrees of sharpness or articulation: how can one affirm that the solution of any such problem is the right one, with absolute certainty? We know how improvised that *première* was, we have read Alan Tyson's speculations about the composer's indecision and haste and we can imagine that second thoughts must have followed. Mr Tyson concludes: 'There is in fact a missing stage, somewhere between the Vienna autograph and the Meyerstein (British Museum) copy, in which the solo violin part was given its final form.'

We have it on the authority of Ries (cited by Thayer) that Beethoven often entrusted piano arrangements of works written for strings to young musicians, whose work he then revised and corrected.

We do not know of any performances of the Concerto after its Vienna *première* (23 December 1806) during the lifetime of Beethoven, except for one in Berlin in 1812 by L. Tomasini. (Those by Baillot, Vieuxtemps, and Ulrich occurred in 1828, 1833 and 1836 respectively.)

There seem to have been no exchanges between composer and performer—after that *première*—that might have led to changes of bowings or revision of details in marks of expression. Thus neither the autograph nor the first edition of the work can be considered a definitive edition, in the sense that a score by Richard Strauss, Debussy, Bartók or Stravinsky represents the last thoughts of these composers. And even these latter, how often did they change details after publication? Bartók, for instance, between the 1931 and the 1944 editions of the Second Rhapsody.

I have seen in the autograph of the Sonata in C minor Op. 30, No. 3, how Beethoven handled one of his 'afterthoughts' in the Finale: he added the eight bars between bars 122 and 130 on a piece of paper sewn on to the manuscript with rough stitches, when it was ready to go to the engraver. And when I was recording Stravinsky's *Duo Concertant* with the composer, using his published *Urtext*, I experienced 'a composer's afterthought' right in the recording studio: he added chords to the violin part in the first movement there and then.

Alfredo Casella (1883–1947), who devoted years of study and research to his edition of the Thirty-two Piano Sonatas, which appeared as early as 1915 (that is, before the Schnabel edition), was revised in 1940 and still commands respect today, has some pertinent things to say about the questions I have been discussing. He is outspoken about the necessity of correcting 'the imperfections of the manuscripts, or of the first editions' and says that he has 'not consented to adopt blindly certain inaccuracies of the manuscripts', thus avoiding 'errors that exist in all the editions'.

'Respect,' writes Casella, 'can never mean the abandonment of critical faculties and a manuscript, though it be Beethoven's, is in no case infallible.'

The Preface from which I quote abounds in references to 'the rapidity and nervous excitability with which Beethoven wrote many of his manuscripts', mentions the dilemma in which the *sf* sign, or the coexistence of three different signs for *staccato*, places us: the *sf* could mean a violent, a strong, moderate, or even soft stressing, the *staccato* could be expressed by commas, dots, and slurred dots.

Again and again Casella mentions the 'haste' and 'feverish nervousness' with which the Master wrote and which led engravers to misinterpret his autograph. It would lead too far to go into the many felicities of Casella's edition in greater detail. However, as I have spoken of Beethoven's 'afterthoughts' (or rather of their absence in the case of the phrasing of the Rondo theme in his Op. 61), let me set down Casella's footnote to the *Adagio e sostenuto* Op. 106 (Hammerklavier Sonata). 'It is not uninteresting to recall that, originally, this *adagio* began with the second bar, and that Beethoven had the present anacrusis (the first bar) added, a few days before its publication.' And it is instructive to compare other editions of the Piano Sonatas with Casella's: Czerny, Steingraber (1888), von Bülow, Schnabel and others.

Scientific methods may solve some of these mysteries; and it is possible that an analysis of the ink might show how the fingering, if fingering it really is, got on to the Vienna autograph of the Rondo. This is something that a mere violinist who has been asked to make a practical edition (not a musicological one, with textual criticism and *Revisionsbericht*!) after playing it for sixty years cannot be expected to do.

Anyway, the 'case' is not yet closed: the State Music Library of Hessen in Darmstadt is preparing a definitive edition for the Beethoven Gesellschaft with photostats, variants, etc. We will know more then.

CHAPTER 23

PLEADS FOR RESPECTFUL ADHERENCE
to Debussy's precise demands for—momentarily
unfashionable—slides between narrow intervals and
incidentally touches upon related subjects

WHEN DEBUSSY marks a *glissando* in the Violin Sonata thus:

Ex. 1

he means just that. To play it in the third position and with a harmonic G is to misjudge the composer's expressive intent and the stylistic 'environment' of the piece.

Ex. 2

is a typically nineteenth century mannerism, whereas when we play it on the D string with the fingering I indicate (the *glissando* that starts with the first finger and with the second finger taking over midway), we achieve the Debussyan '*parlando*' expression and avoid the nineteenth-century '*Morceaux de Salon*' touch that

Ex. 3

inevitably brings to mind.

These two *glissandi* are a comparatively recent type of *portamento-glissando*. The two standard ones are the one with the 'beginning-finger' slide, the other with the 'end-finger' slide. This third type in a way combines the two others by starting with the beginning-finger and letting the end-finger take over in mid-stream. Debussy has indicated unequivocally how he wants these short *glissandi* executed. In marking between

Ex. 4

he made it clear that he had this type of first and second finger slide in mind. This is further borne out by the way he notated the melisma F double sharp in the Finale.

Ex. 5

The F double sharp is in fact a written-out *glissando* of the type I am trying to describe (something easy to demonstrate, but difficult to put across in cold print). It is obvious that the languorousness of this *Le double plus lent* passage demands that it be played on the D string and that the

Ex. 6

and

Ex. 7

should be linked by a singing *glissando* (which this time is not 'written out'). However, in the passage

Ex. 8

it *is* indicated. The same melisma, linking two notes a tone apart is to be found in the first movement (before the recapitulation):

Ex. 9

and

Ex. 10

Also before the coda:

Ex. 11

Observe how the composer makes clear in every case his intention of having these small *glissandi* link the intervals although they are so close together. Exactness of notation really cannot go any further. We find in this score markings like: *sur la touche, cuivré* (for some piano chords), *expressif et soutenu, staccato, expressif et sans rigueur, con fuoco* . . . and still, I confess, I felt the urge to add two more of my own: *parlando* and *Mélisande*.

So many of Debussy's smaller pieces have been transcribed by violinists that it may have escaped the attention of some of us that one of these transcriptions was made by the composer himself: 'Minstrels' from the first book of Preludes.

His meticulous markings and the whole ambience of the piece give us many a clue to his relationship to our instrument, for which he—alas!—wrote so little.

The theme in *pizzicato pp* and marked *vibrez et glissez*, plus a *crescendo* on the F sharp, at once shows how well he recognized the potentialities of the violin generally and *glissandi* (of which we have just spoken *à propos* of the 1917 Sonata) in particular. Left-hand *pizzicati* simultaneously with bowed notes, *sulla tastiera* and *sul ponticello* effects and 'written out' *glissandi* like

Ex. 12

Ex. 13

Ex. 14

show an instrumental imagination that puts to shame many a member of our guild, who seem to lack precisely that quality. Even in such a case I couldn't resist the temptation of adding some touches of my own.

I play instead of

Ex. 15

the same notes but in harmonics

Ex. 16

I also found that the simple device of playing

Ex. 17

open D's instead of

Ex. 18

adds to the intended banjo effect. And I end the piece with the

Ex. 19

played *pizz.* (mixed right and left hand *pizz.* instead of *arco*). All of which is put down here not as a suggestion for imitation, but as an inducement to personal investigation and experimentation in similar situations.

Ravel, who wrote his Violin Sonata between 1923 and 1927, that is some years after Debussy's, used written-out *glissandi* and *pizzicato glissando* effects quite extensively, as did—around the same time—Bartók. In Bartók's Second Sonata (1921), the second movement, bars 25 to 27, we find *glissandi* used to irresistible effect (an effect that has been, by the way, branded 'problematic' by one authority . . .). Webern in his 1910 'Four Pieces' has left-hand *pizzicati* integrated into a fast bowed pattern in a manner so convincing that even the upholders of violinistic 'legitimacy' cannot call it 'problematic'. They seem to forget that while Haydn did not use the sign for *glissandi*, he prescribed it sometimes in an unmistakable manner by his fingerings in the *Urtext*.

In the 1895 Reinhold Jockisch edition of the Haydn Quartet in E flat, Op. 33, No. 2, I find for instance a note in the trio of the Scherzo that 'the fingerings are given here exactly as they are to be found in the first edition'.

Ex. 20

and later

Ex. 21

The fingerings leave no doubt as to the effect Haydn intended: the Viennese lilt! A far cry indeed from the *glissando*-shy manner of our *nouvelle vague* quartet players who for all I know would start this trio in the fourth position and prefer to ignore Haydn's marking of *Sull'istessa corda*. A recent commentator used the words: 'sterile perfectionism' when writing about some performances we hear these days.

To be disdainful about *glissandi* in the above Haydn excerpt is just as ridiculous as it would be to suppress Ravel's *glissandi* in the 'blues' movement of his Sonata in which he wanted to synthetize the New Orleans blues mood.

Ex. 22

Ex. 23

Ex. 24

Ex. 25

CHAPTER 24

BRINGS INTO THE OPEN CERTAIN
rhythmic and tempo distortions which we
tacitly admit and condone

WHEN I TRY to assemble the types of rhythmic distortion to which we
violinists are prone, I am tempted to touch, if only superficially, upon so
many that it is impossible to classify them neatly and illustrate each
deviation with examples. Therefore I will limit myself to those of which I
am most painfully and most often aware.

Outstanding in this 'chamber of horrors' is the distortion of this variation in the Bach Chaconne:

Ex. 1

The passage in demisemiquavers is often played at torrential tempo with
utter disregard of the basic Chaconne rhythm and with an insouciance
which destroys the armature of the whole variation, that is: the $\frac{3}{4}$
rhythm of the quavers, and brings about an unmistakable $\frac{7}{8}$ or $\frac{5}{8}$ time, as
the case may be!

A statement like this may be dismissed with a shrug or an incredulous
snort by those who 'know their Chaconne' and who have never 'noticed

anything wrong' when hearing or playing it. And it is possible that they will call this statement the exaggeration of a pedant—until they put the matter to the test by beating $\frac{3}{4}$ time to it.

Even when the variation can be made to fit into the $\frac{3}{4}$ time (after a fashion) it will probably be through a lengthening and stressing of the melodic bass note sequence at the beginning and end of each bar: D, D–C, C–B flat, B flat–A, and taking a headlong plunge into the whirlpool of the sixteen demisemiquavers until the haven of the bass notes at the end of the bar is reached again! Such is the thoughtlessness of many of our talented violinists who, not having had the *solfeggio* training that their French opposite numbers get as a matter of course, hesitate to probe the dark secrets of a $\frac{3}{4}$ pattern involving one quaver, sixteen demisemiquavers and two semiquavers. In the meanwhile Bach's admirable rhythmic tightening

of the Chaconne tempo of $\frac{3}{4}$ ♩ ♪ | ♩ ♩. ♪ | ♩ into its intensification of

$\frac{3}{4}$ ♪ ♪♩. ♫ | ♪ ♪♩. ♫ | ♪ goes by the board!

No wonder that when the violinist reaches the bar of three groups of semiquavers which precedes the recapitulation of the theme, the lack of rhythmical backbone in this variation takes its revenge: there seems to be no connexion whatsoever, no unity, between the variation and the theme! Such are the consequences of failing to work out this compound metrical figure and 'playing by ear', imitating each other's misconceptions, instead. This kind of thoughtlessness or absence of an analytical approach is at the root of many rhythmic vagaries that convey false impressions.

Who has not heard performances of the last movement of the Brahms D minor Sonata (Op. 108), before the coda, that sound like this?

Ex. 2

The equivocal situation is created by giving in to the temptation of accentuating the 'top note', in this case the B flat, and then being 'short' on the tension-creating three-quavers' rest which precedes the powerful burst of the theme, substituting for this 'composed pause' an indeterminate 'cesura' during which both players glance at each other, wondering which of the two will take the initiative!

A look at the undistorted text:

Ex. 3

will show how far astray a false articulation, a disregard of the composer's phrasing, can lead players and listeners alike. How the absence of that eloquent pause of three quavers can destroy the built-in tension of the six bars leading into the resumption of the theme!

In the opening of the C minor Sonata (Op. 45) by Grieg:

Ex. 4

failure to 'think the $\frac{6}{8}$ rhythm right—that is, in ternary (three times two) terms—will result in the impression of a binary (four times three) rhythm:

Ex. 5

especially if in addition the violinist is guilty of an involuntary accent on the second half of each thematic segment. By enunciating this theme with steady bow pressure and tremendous *élan* on the two halves of each bar, he will convey to the listener the underlying 'twelve to the bar' pulsation, if he 'thinks' it right.

We encounter the same danger in the Saint-Saëns *Rondo Capriccioso* where the violinist's accompaniment figure will clash with the $\frac{6}{8}$ rhythm of the piano if the former does not make it clear that he 'feels' two groups of six semiquavers

Ex. 6

and later:

Ex. 7

and not four groups of triplets:

Ex 8

The same rhythmic ambiguity is found in the *Presto* of Bach's G minor Solo Sonata, which can easily sound like two groups of three or binary, instead of being in ⅜ or ternary tempo:

Ex 9

instead of

Ex 10

Bach's own bowings in passages involving  make the importance

of 'thinking it right' abundantly clear!

An ineffably beautiful piece like the C major Andante from Bach's Solo Sonata in A minor can easily be misunderstood by the hearer in spite of its unmistakable ¾ character. Unless the player is really conscious of its ternary build:

Ex 11

it can easily seem to the listener (who alas! so often hears only beautiful sounds and is little concerned with the gait, the structure of a melody) a binary ⁶⁄₈ melody which I have marked over the top instead of the ternary one which I have marked underneath:

Ex 12

In this case it is the bowing that leads us astray: it needs great subtlety of bow pressure to make clear the three times two subdivision in spite of the 'contradictory' bowing.

*

After dealing with these rhythmic distortions and misunderstandings this is perhaps the place to mention some tempo distortions. Exaggerated slowing down at the passages marked *adagio* just before the coda of the *presto* Finale of the 'Kreutzer' Sonata is a particularly flagrant abuse as it usually bears no relation to the basic *presto* tempo.

Many sonata teams are guilty of a similar disproportionate slowing down eleven and twelve bars before the end of the first movement of the Sonata in A minor, Op. 23. It is as if some players were hypnotized by the word *ritardando* and slow down indiscriminately and without taking into account the context, which in this case is a dramatic Presto movement. They also usually disregard the fact that in this case the *ritardando* is not followed by a pause mark before the *a tempo* nine bars before the end. It is such matters of degree and proportion which make or mar the impact of a performance.

When Beethoven marks *poco adagio* twenty bars before the end of the Sonata Op. 96 he means just that: a '*little* slowly' and not a lachrymose statement of the basically gay *poco allegretto* theme. Besides, this occurs in the concluding *allegro* section of the variation movement, which again means a slowing down in proportion to the *context*. Generally speaking we do not sufficiently take Beethoven 'at his word', when he uses the restrictive term *poco*, as for instance in the Trio Op. 97 (first movement): *poco ritard* for the space of two bars only. One should also guard against misinterpreting his marking *decresc.* by making a simultaneous *rallent.* or *calando* four bars before the *presto* coda in the C minor Sonata Op. 30, No. 2.

At the end of this same Sonata, if I may digress, Beethoven uses a characteristic dynamic marking which is sometimes disregarded: the *ff* towards the climactic end of a movement, reduced to a simple *forte* two bars before the end. At the end of the Piano Sonata Op. 53 ('Waldstein'), he proceeds in the same way: sixth and fifth bars before the end: *pp*; fourth and third bars: *ff*; second but last and last bars: *f*.

To return to the subject of exaggerated slowing down, one of the worst and most generally prevalent offences (of which I too have been guilty in my time) that is known to me is the one committed eleven bars before the end of the Brahms D minor Sonata, Op. 108 (see below).

As the composer wanted to keep in bounds our—natural—inclination to spread out on this last reminiscing restatement of the theme, he warned us not to go beyond a *poco sostenuto* at the critical bars (before the concluding *in tempo*). But we can nowadays hear these four bars inflated to an *adagio* with the piano dying away on a *fermata*, with the result that a bar has in fact been added to this perfectly organized and composed bridge to the concluding *agitato* bars. Such are some distortions that creep into a text and little by little come to be taken for granted.

Undistorted text:

Ex 13

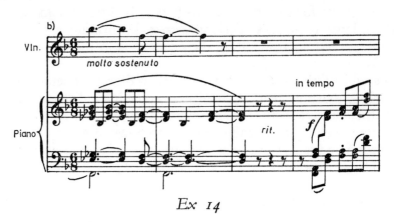

Ex 14

Another such distortion has been fairly generally accepted in the first movement of the Brahms Concerto where, just before the chain of trills that leads into the *tutti* at letter F, the *poco rit.* is nowadays mostly played as a *molto rit.* and, moreover, with the perfectly unwarranted addition of a *fermata* before the *a tempo*.

Ex. 15

The violin works of Brahms seem to be particularly prone to such exaggerations, misunderstandings, unwarranted emendations. Performers either add or subtract, understate or exaggerate. Thus they often choose to ignore the <> sign on the weak beats of the first movement of the D minor Sonata (Op. 108) (the quavers in bars 3, 4, 7 and 8), and pretend to assume that the <> sign concerns the entire bar and not solely this—one might say—'gasping' quaver.

In the G major Sonata Op. 78 one often hears the whole development section (which is marked *più sostenuto* until the recapitulation in *tempo primo* is reached) played without the essential slowing down which the composer —and the shape of the movement!—demands. And this in spite of the warning by Schnabel–Flesch in their edition two bars before the *tempo primo*: '*accelerando,* because preceded by *più sostenuto*'!

In the Adagio of this same Sonata the contrast between the slowness of the Adagio and the—in comparison—markedly more '*gehend*' *Più andante* (which brings us to the recapitulation of the Adagio and the coda) is often insufficiently brought out. A compromise—tempo-wise—with the Adagio played not slowly enough and the *Più andante* not 'marching' enough, can rob this passage, which is the moving centrepiece of the Sonata, of much of its compelling power.

Having heard a recent recording of the Finale of the Brahms Concerto, I am prompted to repeat a few of the remarks I made about this movement in my annotated edition (Curci, Milano), where I advised the student to take the natural articulation of the woodwinds in the first *Tutti* as the model for the enunciation of the principal theme.

Wind players by the very nature of their instruments are safeguarded against the distortion and the sluggishness that results from the violinist's holding on too long on the crotchets in bars 1, 2, 4, 5, and 6. We should model our phrasing at the semiquaver pause on the way the woodwind play the theme during the *Tutti* and try to give a snap to the semiquaver following this pause by playing it at the nut, as if it had a dot above it.

The performance in question was based on an approximate 82 metronome to the crotchet, whereas my 1959 recording is in the neighbourhood of 92–100. In my notes I also warned the student against the excessive slowing down in the last seven bars of the Finale, which is fashionable nowadays but is warranted neither by the score nor by Joachim's edition. The composer has already seen to it that the listener gets the impression of a 'winding-up' process by the descending movement in duple time (of the wind) against the triplet figure of the violin, by the solo violin reverting to duple time five bars before the end (piano) and by the feeling of repose given by the *pizzicatos* in the basses (in crotchets). Why gild the lily?

CHAPTER 25

PROBES THE REASONS WHY A SIMPLE
um-tata accompaniment figure in Beethoven is difficult

W E   A R E inclined to look for problems in obviously complicated passages and sometimes to overlook them in deceptively simple places. Take the opening of Beethoven's Second Sonata (Op. 12, No. 2), than which hardly anything in our literature of masterworks could be more, I would say, embarrassingly simple:

Ex. 1

To tell a student that this accompaniment figure needs thought, fore-sight, practice, critical listening to oneself, would be for the teacher to earn a superior smile from the pupil, who has already tackled tasks like the Tchaikovsky Concerto or the Bach Chaconne.

And still I have heard a very good player 'fall down' on precisely this simple accompaniment figure (in an otherwise superior performance) for reasons that I will enumerate because they will show the reader that there is in our art no such thing as '*quantité négligeable*'.

In the performance I am writing about, the violinist failed to make the bass notes A and B *sound*, thereby taking away the point from Beethoven's witty allocation of the 'um-tata' bass at first to the lyrical instrument—the violin—and the theme to the piano. At this performance the bass notes, being played dryly, with a short downbow bounce and without the ever-so-slight pedal-like emphasis of a small *vibrato*, remained inaudible, thereby depriving the exposition of another facet of Beethoven's witticism: the spice of dissonance given by the 'workaday' bass falling on the inflected 'suspensions' (*Vorhalte*) of the theme in the piano.

Ex. 2

We don't hear ourselves in perspective, so to speak, when we play in *ensemble* combinations; and I dare say the player in question was unaware of this mutilation of the overall (intended) effect. He was not aware that the 'sandy-toned' short downbow bounce was no match in sound balance for the somewhat longer and always more sonorous two upbow notes.

The downbow needed a slight bite besides the above-mentioned *vibrato*. And the whole problem needed a critical listener's evaluating ear!

CHAPTER 26

COMMENTS ON THE PRESENT DISINCLINATION
*to use open strings and deplores the lack of concrete
describable facts about the playing of great figures like
Joachim, Sarasate and others and brings together the little
the author has gathered about some of these*

WE ARE nowadays disinclined to use open strings and this is all to the good
in most cases. But we should deviate from this 'rule' when a naïve tune
demands precisely the simplicity that an extended phrase played on one
string gives. Such a phrase is the exposition of the Andante in the Mendelssohn Concerto of whose first twenty-two bars only four make use of the D
string. In such a context, I find the open A string in

Ex. 1

'in tune' with the perfectly gentle loveliness of the long melody.
   Another such phrase occurs in Schubert's Sonatina Op. 137, No. 2

Ex. 2

Is it inability to play it with the innocent beauty it demands (play it entirely
on the E string!) that is the cause of its rare appearance on our programmes?

It is disquieting to see the Mendelssohn called in print (in 1966) 'the by no means evergreen Mendelssohn Concerto' and to notice how rarely, if ever, competitors at international competitions choose it for the 'finals', where they have free choice.

When Carl Flesch, in 1928, published the second volume of his *Art of Violin Playing*, he was still able to call the Mendelssohn Concerto 'the most popular' of its kind. This no longer holds good today.

Is it not because they cannot do justice to the Mendelssohn that our young players shun this test?

As a boy, when I played the Mendelssohn Concerto I took the A in the second bar of the Andante theme as a harmonic according to the—then still living—tradition, something that is hardly ever done nowadays. This still seems to me today in keeping with the *'lied'*-like understated character of the narrative that only later develops into something more personally involved.

The following reminiscings of Sir George Henschel about Sarasate's playing of the Mendelssohn at the 1877 Nether-Rhenish Music Festival therefore seemed to me like a confirmation of a vague supposition. (The book, *Musings and Memories of a Musician*, published by Macmillan & Co. Ltd. in 1918, is a recent lucky find during one of my habitual browsings outside secondhand booksellers.) Sir George wrote: '. . . Spain, too, was represented by one of her most famous sons, the matchless Pablo de Sarasate. His interpretation of the Mendelssohn Concerto came to German ears like something of a revelation, creating a veritable furore, and indeed I doubt if in lusciousness of tone, crystalline clearness of execution, refinement and grace that performance has been or ever will be surpassed. Alone the way he took that little A natural, the fifth note of the *Andante* theme, without letting the string touch the fingerboard—*'sur la touche'* I think is the technical term for it—gave one a thrill of artistic joy never to be forgotten.'

I give this quotation despite its rather tentative description of a simple

Ex. 3

harmonic, because we today must be grateful for any scrap of information that comes our way, when it concerns something as ephemeral as perform-ance tradition of ninety years ago.

My own memories of Sarasate's playing a year or two before his passing (1908) are so dim that I hesitate to set them down. It may have been my immaturity or a lack of concentration on my part but I retain nothing characteristic about that afternoon recital at Wigmore Hall in London except his fixed gaze beyond the heads of the audience and a feeling that he was somehow absent from and not deeply involved in the music. This 'fixed gaze' may have been due to physical causes: the portraits that were given to me in his birthplace, Pamplona, in 1908, where I was soloist at the annual Fiesta de San Fermin, show protuberant eyes, that probably were falsely interpreted by the callow youth I was at the time of Sarasate's Wig-more Hall recital. His recording of the Bach Prelude in E (made some five years before his death) is in such contradiction to everything a Carl Flesch or a W. J. Wasielewski says about Sarasate's exemplary intonation, techni-cal polish and other virtues that I prefer to let the reader form his own opinion by listening to this recently available historical disc. But to be able to listen to 'historical' recordings of the first decade of our century (or even later) with profit, it is necessary that the listener's historical sense enters into play.

Sir George Henschel had heard Sarasate in 1877, I had heard him in 1906 or possibly 1907. That is the crucial difference. The change in taste, in violinistic *Weltanschauung*, has to be taken into account. Thanks to Carl Flesch we know a little about the meteoric ascent of Sarasate, about his comparatively early decline and his 'unrequited love'—as Flesch calls it—for chamber music.

A glimpse of Sarasate's love of quartet playing comes from an un-expected source: from Jean Cocteau, who in his *Portraits-Souvenir* (1900–14) describes how Sarasate played quartets with Cocteau's grandfather, a wealthy amateur, how he held forth about his 'conquests in Europe' and how proudly he showed the tiny golden violin, complete with case, that the Queen of Spain had presented to him and that he wore on a gold chain.

What do we know about the concrete, describable facets of Paganini's playing in spite of dozens of biographies, in spite of Berlioz', Liszt's, Heine's testimonies? And what will the student and his teacher of, say, 1980, know about Kreisler's playing of the Elgar Concerto in 1910? What does the author of one of the most widely distributed (I won't say 'read'!)

books about our instrument and its practitioners mean, when he writes about Fritz Kreisler: '. . . (he) acquired an elegant but deep [*sic*] intonation from Massart'? We also read in this book that Willy Burmester (1869–1933) practised the Paganini C major Caprice 'no less than 4,276 times', and other information of similar importance.

On the other hand we see that a *vibrato*-less, pure harmonic A heard in 1877 haunts a distinguished musician's memory (Sir George Henschel was the first conductor the Boston Symphony Orchestra ever had, when it started on its now century-old career) when he assembles his autobiographical writings some time before the First World War.

Such is the power of a supposedly non-essential 'small' touch in a performance.

I had the rare privilege of hearing Leopold Auer in December 1913 in St Petersburg when he played the Beethoven Concerto under Willem Mengelberg's direction. He himself commented on this performance in a letter to his pupil Kathleen Parlow, the Canadian violinist (1890–1963), in these words: '. . . for instance, I played here the Beethoven a week ago and people did find I never have done it so well—think in my age!' (From *Kathleen Parlow* by Maida Parlow French, the Ryerson Press, Toronto, 1967.)

I am reluctant to set down my own rather less positive—though admittedly vague—memories of this courageous deed on the part of a master nearing seventy. Of course my youthful unreasonableness must have been responsible for my feeling of disappointment and frustration: I must have expected—without formulating this expectation to myself, of course!—the teacher of Elman, Heifetz, Zimbalist (all of whom I had heard by that time) to outdo them all, not only in the indefinable qualities of wisdom, style and 'format' but also in tone, technical perfection and *élan*.

This juvenile anticipation was of course absurd; the robustness of Mengelberg's orchestral frame only emphasized the thinness and carefulness of the obviously nervous old master's playing. (When, on his way to the podium, he caught sight of me sitting behind the orchestra, he chaffed me about my youth and about his courage in facing *this* challenge at his age.) In fact, paradoxically enough, the characteristics of the 'Auer School', or rather of what these extraordinary young virtuosi have led us to consider its characteristics, were just what I missed in Auer's playing.

With hindsight can we not ask ourselves whether our conception of the Auer School does not owe its existence to the unique and individually differentiated gifts of this triumvirate (Elman, Heifetz, Zimbalist) rather than to some 'new approach' on the part of the master himself? Even the so-called 'Russian bowhold' which Carl Flesch attributes to Auer (or rather to his outstanding disciples) does not seem to represent Auer's intentions entirely. The recently published A. Moser–Nösselt *Geschichte des Violinspiels* (Vol. II, Hans Schneider, Tutzing bei München, 1967) points out that in Auer's *Graded Course of Violin Playing* (Carl Fischer, New York, 1926) he advocates the 'Old' 'Campagnoli bowhold' (fingers close together on the stick) and not the so-called 'Russian' one that (rightly or wrongly) bears his name!

The neat 'genealogical tables' showing how twentieth-century violinists descend from this or that illustrious 'chef d'École' of the past are not as dependable as the authors of these books would like to make them seem. Even 'the rare privilege' of hearing some great representative of our art—in his declining years, it must be added—does not always enable the listener to pass on to future generations impressions that fix the place and rank and distinguishing features of players who belong to the history of violin-playing.

CHAPTER 27

GIVES A GLIMPSE OF HOW CRITICALLY
and with what reluctance the vibrato—*now indispensable—*
was regarded around the middle of the nineteenth century,
and supplements the preceding chapter with some
impressions of Joachim's playing

Now LET me give an example of this change in *Weltanschauung* pertaining to one facet of our art, the *vibrato*.

When the cellist A. F. Servais (1807–66), one of the founders—along with Ch. de Beriot—of the Belgian School of String Playing, appeared in 1835 in London, he was criticized (in the *Athenæum*) for the 'unusual manner of producing his tone' by 'that intense pressure of the fingers' which has since been better understood by the term *"vibrato"*, and this was at once denounced to be 'spasmodic and a not altogether creditable trick'. And following this, Servais' playing was unfavourably compared to that of the English cellist Lindley, who 'brought out all his tone like the rolling notes of an organ' and whose tone 'being always smooth, there was no tremulousness whatever apparent in his playing'.

After these denunciations of our *vibrato* let us set down here a pondered description of this phenomenon by an acoustic scientist (who used to be an orchestral violinist). He calls it 'a rapid fluctuation of pitch at the same loudness' and adds that it 'contributes an unmistakable human and living quality to musical sound'.

These two descriptions (1835 and 1966) are of course extreme examples of the change tastes undergo. But whenever I let colleagues or pupils listen to recordings of Ysaÿe or Huberman, I warn them not to judge these by the standard prevalent today and to take into account certain idiosyncrasies rooted in the 'Zeitgeist'.

One of Eugène Ysaÿe's biographers (the other being his son Antoine)

173

tells how Eugène's father Nicolas—who was his first teacher—admonished him at the age of five or six with a furious 'What! you already use *vibrato*? I forbid you to do so! You are all over the place like a bad tenor. *Vibrato* will come later, and you are not to deviate from the note. You'll *speak* through the violin.' This was in 1863 or 1864 approximately; and listening to the beautiful, chaste, close *vibrato* on his 1912 Columbia U.S.A. recording I feel that this paternal admonition bore fruit in Ysaÿe's *unthrobbing* lovely *cantilena* as I still remember it. Who knows how our universally praised recordings will sound to turn of the twenty-first century ears?

I never heard Joachim (although I did play to him in 1905 at the time of my premature Berlin début), and therefore I always regretted that no one had tried to describe at least some facets of his playing by reference to concrete facts instead of rhapsodizing about it. Even Bruno Walter's autobiography, *Theme and Variations*, fails to give us his impressions as a young musician of Joachim's playing of the Beethoven Concerto. (We may assume this performance to have taken place in the late 1880s or early nineties, when Joachim was in his fifties or sixties.) Bruno Walter does speak in some detail about a quartet performance shortly before Joachim's death in 1907, when the 'simplicity and greatness' of the aged master's playing, whose 'hand and intonation were no longer reliable' made a deep, ineradicable impression on the conductor who was later to achieve such greatness.

Otto Klemperer's student memories of Joachim's playing in Beethoven quartets give us a somewhat more concrete idea of what his playing must have been like: 'When he was not bothered by nervousness he played in a manner that carried one away. The last movement of the C sharp minor Quartet for instance he played like a fiery Hungarian fiddler, not at all in the "classical manner".'

Even a violinist who studied with Joachim, like Sam Franko, disappoints our expectations. In 1879 he heard Joachim in the Brahms Concerto (it was its first performance in Berlin) and all he has to say about it in his memoirs (*Chords and Discords*, Viking Press, New York, 1938), is that the work 'made no impression at all' and that Joachim was so nervous that, in order to calm himself, he played the first violin part of Mendelssohn's overture 'Fingal's Cave', while standing at the back at the last desk. However, in justice to Sam Franko I must add that he does attempt to give the reader a description of sorts, when he writes: 'Joachim's tone did not dazzle and flatter the hearer by means of penetrating sensuousness. It was a tone whose limpid beauty had a transcendental quality. His playing was spiritualized and etherealized. There was no coquetry, no seeking after effect. To speak of Joachim as quartet player would be to "carry fiddles to Cremona". The freedom of his interpretation and technical superiority, the *élan* of his playing and his phrasing—all mark him out as the greatest interpreter of his kind. Joachim gave us something which has scarcely ever before been presented in such perfection and which it is hard to imagine will ever come again.'

Sir George Henschel, to whom we owe that glimpse of Sarasate's playing of the Mendelssohn in Chapter 26, is more reticent about that of Joachim, whom he often heard and accompanied in the years when the violinist was at the apex of his powers. All we learn is that, during the summer holiday he spent with the Joachims in 1874 in the Austrian Alps, he accompanied him in Joachim's Hungarian Concerto and those of Beethoven, Mendelssohn and Spohr, and in Sonatas by Locatelli, Tartini and Handel, that he practised every day for some time, that he was an excellent walker, often starting at five o'clock in the morning, and other information of a like nature. But little of what we violinists hope for. . . .

Nor does Sir Henry Wood's description of the diamond jubilee of Joachim in London in May 1904, which he had conducted and at which Joachim played the Beethoven Concerto, bring us even a glimpse of what this 'memorable performance' (Sir Henry's only comment) was like. Mr Balfour who was president of this festive occasion, referred to the then thirteen-year-old Joachim's performance of the same Concerto at the Philharmonic Concert of 27 May 1844 under Mendelssohn's direction. Is it surprising that a performance sixty years later evoked from the thirty-five-year-old conductor only the obviously evasive comment of 'memorable'? And that if we read on in Sir Henry's *My Life of Music* (Victor Gollancz, 1938) we find the same disinclination to commit himself about the playing of the seventy-three-year-old master? He writes: 'Of Joachim I always felt that one was in the presence of a Hungarian gentleman of great intellect, and although his playing lacked the emotional depth of that of dear Ysaÿe his was a quiet classical serenity free from any trace of exaggeration and always musical and scholarly.'

When the writer speaks of Lady Hallé's playing (Wilma Neruda-Hallé was considered the best woman violinist at the turn of the century) he gives us—indirectly—his true feelings about Joachim. He writes: 'The nobility of her style reminded me of Joachim but, to be quite candid, I thought her tone more musical than his; certainly her intonation was better.'

More evocative for us today are the lines that the Berlin music critic Dr Julius Levin (by vocation a practising physician) wrote in the German monthly *Die Musik* in 1926. This writer had heard Joachim in 1883 for the first time and summed up his impressions in the word 'inimitable', which he used time and again. He speaks about the ethereal and 'sublimating spiritual' quality of Joachim's tone and of his way with whatever music he touched, but mentions also the 'purely sensuous force' of his expressive sonority. What strikes one who today tries to piece together these 'scraps of information' is the stress the writer puts on the 'unique propelling power' of Joachim's playing and about his capacity to use those passages (I presume he is referring to Beethoven's later Quartets) that 'go against the grain', to further his own expressive aims. This seems to me a key sentence in the reminiscings, as is also his quoting one of Joachim's quartet associates as saying: 'To play with him is damned difficult. Always different tempi, different accents . . .' This leads Julius Levin to ruminate about the demoniac, the improvising element in Joachim's make-up.

A far cry indeed from the mental picture we have had of the great man on the basis of the writings of Victorian critics, on the basis of suppositions, of editions that carry his name, but were published only a very few years before his death. . . . Nor must we give too much weight to G. B. Shaw's review of Joachim's playing of the Bach Fugue in C in 1890 quoted on p. 126. A great player's scattered performances quite naturally leave contradictory and inconclusive memories behind.

CHAPTER 28

CONCERNS A BOWING DEVICE VARIOUSLY
called 'reprise de l'archet', *the* 're-taking' *of the bow,*
and by other names, which enhances the speaking quality of
certain phrase fragments

IT IS difficult to draw the line between what is a full realization of a musical text and what is downright amendment, that is, changing of the text. Every full realization of the implications of a text is already an 'arrangement', an amendment. To apply a *'reprise d'archet'*, where one can get by without it, for instance in various passages with dotted crotchets or quavers or:

Ex. 1

is already—technically speaking—a change. To draw the bow practically full length, quit the string swiftly and inaudibly *above* the string and return the upper (or lower, as the case may be) quarter, or less, of the bow to the string, that is: *'reprendre'* the bow, is a complicated-sounding procedure that adds inches to the bow and eloquence and meaning to the phrase (provided that the *'reprendre'* is appropriate to it, of course). And this enhancement cannot be measured in inches.

In doing this we will have realized what the composer in many cases heard with his inner ear but did not notate as he took it for granted that the violinist (or other string player) would, as a matter of course, break the flow —just as any woodwind player does with the tongue—between the dotted note and the quaver or semiquaver. This procedure used to come as naturally to distinguished string players of a few decades ago as 'speaking prose'

177

came to Monsieur Jourdain! Brahms took it for granted when he put the dot on the E in the opening bar of the Violin Concerto:

Ex. 2

and so did Tartini for the *Largo* of the G minor *Didone Abbandonata*:

Ex. 3

If we look at some of the bowings which Adolf Busch advocated in his editions and if we retain memories of the eloquence and natural breathing of his playing, we will realize how little aware we were of this 'enhancement' at the time. And the inconspicuousness of this procedure (which nowadays seems so complicated to the rank and file of our players) shows how 'naturally' it came to its practitioners.

Bach Chaconne

Ex. 4

Bach–Busch Sonata in G major

Ex. 5

178

Bach Sonata No. 6 in G major for Clavier and Violin

Ex. 6

Vitali Chaconne

Ex. 7

Brahms Sonata in G major Op 78

Ex. 8

and

Ex. 9

Bach Sonata No. 6 in G for Clavier and Violin

Ex. 10

Corelli–Léonard La Follía

Ex. 11

Ernest Bloch 'Nigun'

Ex. 12

All this does not mean that I consider the *reprise de l'archet* the only way of doing justice to these passages; the usual way of playing them nowadays—that is, without expending the bow to the extent that I in my own playing have considered desirable, without retaking it from approximately its starting point—*can* do justice to the letter. But whether it can convey the spirit is a moot point.

So little has been written about this traditional adjunct to our 'arsenal' that I thought it right to make this digression, give a few examples and enable the reader to experiment with both ways of playing them. It is my hope that the experiment will prove the expressive advantage there is in using the bow in this lavish way rather than in the usual somewhat skimped 'economical' manner.

CHAPTER 29

IN WHICH THE AUTHOR TRIES HIS HAND
at a definition of what he means by 'enhancement',
incidentally invoking memories of Ysaÿe and Kreisler

WHENEVER I find something that I rightly or wrongly feel to be an enhancement of a given text, I think of a somewhat eccentric, fastidious musician friend of my youth with whom I sometimes used to play some fifty years ago, who occasionally presented to me pianistic *'trouvailles'*, with a gleam in his eye, like a gourmet challenging you to guess what ingredients went into some very special dish! He used to speak of *'de luxe'* fingerings and the like. Of nuances really too fine for and therefore wasted on, the uninitiated. . . . I sometimes suspect myself of being somewhat quirky too; for instance, when I tell a pupil or a younger colleague: 'why not a harmonic D just after the cadenza of the Tchaikovsky Concerto that will ring like a celesta and give a harmony "envelope" to the *legato fioritura*?'

Ex. 1

or: 'Why not give the bass notes in the Bach A minor Fugue the booming sound of the G string?'

Ex. 2

Or: 'How about using that same harmonic D which served us so well in the Tchaikovsky, towards the end of the—I know, very dissimilar!—Beethoven Concerto last movement, after the unexpected turning to A flat? The pure bell-like ring will beautifully prepare that pastoral entry of the oboe, just eight bars away.'

When Ysaÿe ended this passage in the Bach E major Concerto's last movement with a trumpet-like fanfare on the G string

Ex. 3

it was truly a '*de luxe*' fingering that he used instead of the comfortably traditional one; it involved a contortion of his amazingly flexible fourth finger between D sharp and G sharp.

Sometimes it is the very exertion in bringing off some feat that enhances a passage. And to do it in Bach is by no means incongruous. Aren't his Solo Sonatas full of such challenges?

Another such 'unnecessary' expenditure of dazzling virtuosity was lavished by Ysaÿe right at the beginning of the B minor Concerto of Saint-Saëns which he played with this fingering because it took advantage of the chordal sweep across the four strings with incomparable effect.

Ex. 4

This passage can perfectly well be played in the first position, but Ysaÿe liked to 'live dangerously'!

Kreisler's bowing in this passage in the first movement of the Mozart Concerto K. 218

Ex. 5

though it cannot be called dangerous, was so irresistibly idiomatic, something so much his own, that it stamped itself into one's consciousness to the extent that passage and execution became an indivisible whole. The unorthodox jump of the upbow from C sharp to G sharp gave it a snap, a virile grace that one felt could not be attained in any other way. This is what I called the unmistakable 'handwriting' of instrumentalists (in the Introduction). When in the G major *Musette* in the *Rondeau* of the same Concerto he held on to the

Ex. 6

drone while the orchestra *tutti* responded to the solo, thus reinforcing the bagpipe effect of oboes, cellos and basses, it was utterly convincing—but only in the context of the Kreisler projection of the whole. I don't advocate it to those who seek my opinion today. Whatever he touched acquired the Kreisler touch and when comparing his emendations with the original, one remained convinced of the rightness of his instinct; as, for example, when he inverted the order of the twice-played theme of Debussy's *La Fille aux Cheveux de Lin* (in A. Hartmann's 'composer-approved' transcription) playing it first in stopped notes and only at the repeat in harmonics (instead of the other way round).

CHAPTER 30

GIVES EXAMPLES OF OTHER ENHANCEMENTS
to show what can be done to attain a fuller realization of
the composer's implied intentions that cannot always be
defined on the printed page

FROM SUCH refinements of execution it is only a step to explore other ways in which a text, or rather the implications of a text can be realized. Although Ravel's notation of the *Perpetuum mobile* of his Sonata is:

Ex. 1

he was perfectly in accord with me when I played it with him with this bowing:

Ex. 2

Prokofiev willingly accepted my suggestion of reinforcing certain hammered out notes in his Concerto No. 1 (Scherzo), by doubling them (*Unisono*) and I quite naturally used this same brash-sounding device at the end of the first movement of his Solo Sonata Op. 115. When later I read that this work was written not for a lone violin, but for a *group* of violinists for a music school performance, I felt elated at having had this 'hunch', for these *unisono* notes precisely give the symbolic, even though not the actual effect of an ensemble of violins.

Béla Bartók was in wholehearted agreement with me when I showed him that the dance theme of the second part ('Friss') of his first Rhapsody (1928)

Ex. 3

should be played mostly on two strings, in order to bring out the 'folk-fiddler' quality of the tune, instead of with the normal, comfortable fingering marked underneath, which makes of it something citified, lacking in precisely the character he was aiming for and which is implicit in the whole movement. Its sub-title is 'Folk Dances'. Moreover it uses the *cimbalom* in its orchestral version and generally breathes this folk-music, outdoor atmosphere. The unprejudiced listener will barely notice what contortions were necessary to play it my way because it will sound so right, so inevitable. But it invariably raises the eyebrows of the professional when I show it to one of these. . . . This is to be expected.

It is surprising to me how often the chordal passage in Bartók's Rhapsody No. 1 (at No. 13) is misunderstood in spite of its unmistakable notation.

Ex. 4

The theme being on the middle string (D) the player has to *aim* at the D string and trust to his expertise in weight distribution that the adjacent strings will respond to the pressure of his index finger and of his bow-arm as it aims horizontally at the D string. It is as simple as that. (I have tried to make it still more explicit by my markings.)

But the comparative neglect in our early studies of means to acquire real bowing mastery (as distinct from fast *spiccato, staccato* and the like) makes a passage like this redoubtable. It is what Bach demands in the sixth and seventh bars of the Adagio of the C major Solo Sonata in the Fugue and in several other places. Of course the present 'fashion' of arpeggiating chords downward in Bach Fugues as at:

Ex. 5

has contributed to the incapacity of our bow-arm to cope with such chordal problems.

Bartók is being paid lip-service these days when he is so much in vogue. But is he being paid the tribute violinists owe him by using those forty-four Duos for Two Violins as he meant them to be used? (How illogical to attempt to play the two Rhapsodies without the background information which these Duos give to the Western musician. Attempting to do this is rather in the nature of taking a short cut.)

Even an accomplished string player like Hindemith did not say all that could be said in marking his Solo Sonata Op. 31, No. 2. This outstand-ingly attractive and rewarding work has a third movement that is played throughout *pizzicato*. I suggest that the student tackles these twenty-eight bars first in the traditional way, that is, *pizzicato* with right hand. (The composer does not specify any left-hand ones.) Then let him (or her) experiment with these suggestions of interspersed left hand *pizzicati*:

Bar
 1: left hand on 2nd quaver of bar
 4: left hand on 1st and 2nd quaver
 6: left hand on last semiquaver (F)
 7: left hand on both Fs and B flat and G flat
13: left hand on E, A and D sharp and G sharp

186

15: left hand on the three Bs
17: as Bar 1
20: left hand on 1st and 2nd quaver by sliding from E to A
21: as Bar 1
22: as Bar 1
28: left hand on last note *ppp* B flat

Avoid open A string in last three bars.

The composer does not indicate a metronome number but specifies *Gemäch-liche Viertel* (comfortably calm crotchets). I suggest approximately 84–8.

By alternating the plucking finger, and by sometimes using the thumb, in Ravel's *Tzigane,* for instance:

Ex. 6

one can make *pizzicato* effects more effective and easier.

Thus at the end of the first movement of Prokofiev's Second Concerto

Ex. 7

I often find that a certain adventurousness is needed to bring off some *pizzicato* effects that composers imagine, but that fail to materialize with orthodox means. So nine bars before the end of the *Allegro brusco* of Prokofiev's Sonata in F minor Op. 80, the climactic *pizzicato* chord

Ex. 8

will not sound sufficiently biting because the plucking first finger will naturally have given more power to the lower strings than to the F on the E string. I try to remedy this by arpeggiating the *pizzicato,* using the four plucking fingers in the succession: 4, 3, 2, 1. In this way F is assured of sufficient sound and the effect is more that of a simultaneous chord than of an arpeggiated one.

Bartók, notably in his String Quartets, wished in some cases to achieve a hard snapping sound, instead of the usual plucking effect. He had to invent a new musical sign **ö** in order to make clear that he wanted to have the string *lifted* by two fingers off the fingerboard, letting it rebound with precisely this 'hard snapping sound', as it has been described by a commentator of the Quartets. Another unorthodox *pizzicato* device of Bartók's is the following: from his String Quartet No. 4.

Ex. 9

and

Ex. 10

Claudio Monteverdi (1567–1643) is supposed to have been the first to use violin *pizzicato*. He gave the instruction: 'Here one leaves off playing with the bow, and the strings are to be plucked with two fingers.' One wonders whether this does not mean something like the Bartókian hard snapping sound. (Of course it may be that Monteverdi had two *alternating* plucking fingers in mind.)

In the Mendelssohn Concerto during transition from the cadenza to the arpeggios, I used to double the bass in order to have the benefit of two open strings, also in order to have the sweep across all four strings sooner and the radiance of the moving voice on the E string instead of on the A string (as in the second example):

Ex. 11

Thus several objectives were attained by one easy change from the usual procedure.

Ex. 12

Sometimes it is 'things not worth mentioning' that make quite a difference at some strategic point, like the unison D eighteen bars before the end of Szymanowski's *Fontaine d'Aréthuse*. I play it as a wavy *bariolage* line in a way that resembles a *vibrato* brought forth by the undulating bow. (A very unsatisfactory description, this!)

CHAPTER 31

MORE OF THE SAME, BUT WITH PARTICULAR
emphasis on bowing problems

MASTERY OF the bow—words of great portent, even though we do nowadays refrain from writing 'bow' with a capital B, or speaking about the 'Soul of the Bow' as some used to in the 1920s.

But aren't we faced with the necessity of this mastery at every meaningful turn of a phrase, at every figuration, if it is to be more than just empty decorative tinsel? It is not the marvellously light and fast *spiccato* that has become a commonplace in our days in pieces of the Paganini *Moto perpetuo*, or the 'Flight of the Bumble Bee' type, nor is it the capacity to reel off the first Paganini Caprice ('*Arpeggio*' E major) with a faultlessly functioning, bouncing bow that constitutes mastery. Ask this player to lead into the *arpeggios* that follow the cadenza in the Mendelssohn Concerto

Ex. 1

by playing the downward group with slow, propelled upbow, flying *staccato,* and only gradually reach the automatically bouncing *arpeggio* (four bars before the orchestra enters) and we will see the extent of control his bow-arm is capable of.

Ask him to give minute inflections on the thematically moving parts in Bach's E major Prelude

Ex. 2

against the background of the open E-s or to do the same in the Mozart Concerto K. 218

Ex. 3

and his bow-arm, though capable of vertiginous *spiccato* speed, will respond rather inadequately.

Criticize him for not giving more prominence to the melodic line than to the accompaniment in the *Andante* of the Mendelssohn Concerto,

Ex. 4

the similar passage in Ysaÿe's Solo Sonata No. 3,

Ex. 5

or this passage from the cadenza of the Glazunoff Concerto,

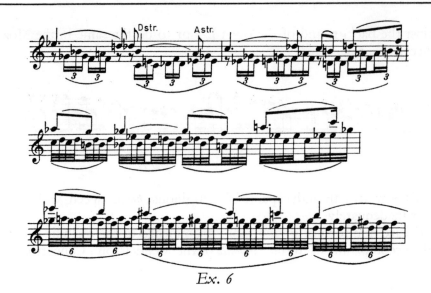

Ex. 6

and he will probably prove somewhat inexpert in the technique of distributing the weight of his bow unequally between the upper, melodic, and the lower, accompanying, string.

These slow double-stop *tremolos* that accompany a tune have been called 'a problem that only very few players can solve'. So let us see whether my suggestion of practising them in the following manner will help to solve this discouraging problem. While practising give the utmost attention and intensity to the melodic (upper) part, while playing the accompaniment *mute*, that is, without the bow sounding the lower string.

This is the first step towards our goal: to realize that it is the shifts, the wriggling between positions of the *tremolo* accompaniment that causes the unsatisfactory *vibrato*-less, faulty intonation of our melodic line!

Once we have conquered this difficulty, we can proceed to the 'cleaning up' and the smooth joining of the *tremolo* segments and now apply the inverse practise method: concentrate on the accompaniment figure and finger the melody mute without the bow touching the upper string. Another practice phase can of course be the relatively loud playing of the melody and a barely audible *tremolo* accompaniment.

The goal may still be a long way off, but at least we will know that we are on the right track and that this procedure will help us in many similar cases, as, for instance, in the variation of the Beethoven G major *Romanze* (at the recapitulation), in the beautiful G minor Caprice by Paganini and elsewhere.

When I point out to such a player the advantages of playing the lower bowing in the last movement of Handel's D major Sonata, from the third to the eleventh bar

Ex. 7

instead of the conventional upper bowing, he will be in favour of 'playing safe' and using the traditional bowing, which not only is less rhythmically articulate but inevitably monotonous with its sixteen repeats of the same formula: sixteen down bows, sixteen upbows in a row.... The force of habit and the prestige of the printed page is such that he will disregard these advantages and prefer not to spend thought and practice time on a

swift lifting of the bow at the nut (after the ♩♩♩♩♩) and a corresponding

elegant lifting ♩♩♩♩♩ at the tip of the bow in the second halves of the bars.

Thus, for the sake of comfort, he will forgo the musical enhancement that results from alternation in sequential passages.

The superstition of 'downbow on every strong beat' is still with us. Take the *Corrente* of the D minor Partita by Bach: to play the three groups of triplets as these are noted in the MS. and as they are generally played, that is, the first note downbow, the remaining eight notes upbow, will inevitably bring an imbalance into the sequence. The single note on the downbeat will be too long and too loud; the absence of alternation will make for monotony.

By separating the first note from the eight (on the *same* bow)

Ex. 8

193

we are faithful to the spirit of the text, avoid the insistent over-accented downbows, reap the benefit of alternation. Kreisler used this same bowing in the Mozart G major *Rondo*:

Ex. 9

The discipline imposed by this articulation at the nut and the point of the bow will in addition be a valuable study.

To liberate ourselves from the superstitious notion that upbow has to follow downbow, let us take a close look at the second movement of Bach's Third Violin and Clavier Sonata:

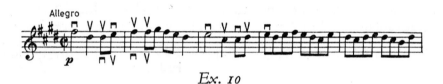

Ex. 10

which in my minority opinion gains considerably by the unorthodox (upper) bowing; it avoids the involuntary stress on the F sharp of the second bar and thus leaves the minims (F sharp and E) their full significance. As there are four F sharps in the first couple of bars and five E's in the next two bars, vigilance is needed if we are to avoid redundancy and preserve the winged lightness of the theme. The two minute liftings (at the point of the bow) will come naturally to a well-equipped light bow-arm and the following third and fourth bars (played with the orthodox ⊓V⊓V bowing) will give the theme the right complementary 'weight'. To make my meaning clear: it will be perceived by the listener somewhat like this:

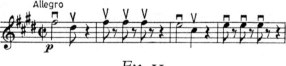

Ex. 11

194

Two consecutive downbows and upbows can render good services to articulation generally, as in the variation of the *Giga* of the Pisendel Solo Sonata in A minor where

Ex. *12*

will give the sequence an incisiveness that  could not give. All these bowings presuppose a lightness and suppleness of the bow-arm, the lack of which George Szell deplores in the letter I quoted in Chapter 10. Therefore it will not surprise me if the foregoing suggestions and those that follow will be shrugged off by some as unnecessary and risky (or unnecessarily risky!).

For instance, my idea that an involuntary downbow stress can be avoided in the fourth bar of the Rondo theme of the Beethoven Concerto, by playing

Ex. *13*

instead of with the lower bowing. (An almost imperceptible lifting of the bow will be necessary between the two upbows.) Or that *sforzandi* need not necessarily be played downbow. Witness the first movement of the Beethoven Sonata Op. 30, No. 3

Ex. *14*

where my avoiding of downbows on the strong beats of the second and fourth bars will lend added weight to the two *sforzandi,* where they are needed—in the sixth bar.

By using the lower bowing my feeling is that we are weakening the effect of these concluding and conclusive *sforzandi* prematurely. In the theme of the Rondo of Beethoven's Sonata Op. 12, No. 3, I avoid the danger of an involuntary accent on the unaccented third bar by playing

Ex. 15

so as not to weaken the impact of the *sforzandi.*

CHAPTER 32

STILL MORE PAGES ON THE INEXHAUSTIBLE
subject of bowing mastery, with some examples of bowings
that are generally supposed to 'go against the grain'

AT A TIME like ours when the average violinist's equipment is at an unprecedented high level and teaching and know-how are systematized as
never before, it may sound paradoxical when I say that there seems to be
—at least to me!—a regression in the use of the bow for effects that are far
beyond the ordinary.

The swift downbow after a long upbow (something rather against the
'rules'!) that was done as a matter of course in the Finale of the Mendelssohn when I studied it is nowadays often avoided and replaced by the
lower, uncharacteristic bowing.

Ex. 1

This gasp-like quaver was handed down to us through Joachim, Sarasate,
Hubay, but seems to be thought a superfluous refinement today. (The
notation in the score authenticates this tradition.) We find this swift downbow also in the D minor Sonata of Brahms Op. 108 right at the beginning
(where the less expressive lower bowing, however, *can* be substituted for
it).

Ex. 2

It is probably the element of risk that keeps players from 'fulfilling' themselves in phrases like these: these swift downbows can of course sometimes result in a whistling sound, but the risk is worth taking. Such expressive enhancements cannot easily be conveyed in cold print, any more than can Caruso's or other Italian tenors' 'sob' at the climactic end of a cadence.

There are, however, signs that the process of making daring passages 'safe' (safe for microphones!) is now being abandoned for more faithful adherence to the original text. For instance at the Moscow Tchaikovsky Competition, where the Tchaikovsky Concerto is of course obligatory, only the original version by the author may be used. Thus the simplification of the redoubtable passage in triplets (in sixths) by L. Auer (who reduced it to single notes) is no longer admitted and we now hear it in the exciting dry *spiccato* or else *'fouetté' detaché* double-stop original version, the way Huberman (and before him Brodsky and others) used to play it. I too adhered to the original in my time. I ceased to play the Concerto in 1925.

Ex. 3

Today's student who takes for granted this fascinating and inspired work will read with incredulity of the heartbreak it caused the composer. There was first Auer's refusal to play it; then Hanslick's vitriolic blast at its Vienna *première* by Adolf Brodsky; the riotous demonstration against it; the fact that Auer apparently dissuaded Emile Sauret from playing it and 'intrigues against it' (Tchaikovsky's letter to his publisher of 16 January 1882). Auer later recanted and became one of its champions by teaching it to his phenomenally gifted pupils around the turn of the century. In an article published in 1912 he 'explains' his early refusal and his subsequent editorial changes or simplifications (whichever one likes to call them) by saying that he found 'some of the passages were not suited to the character of the instrument'.

And now the Soviet school of violin playing reinstates the Concerto in its original state, rejects all editorial changes and so-called emendations by insisting that competitors at the Tchaikovsky Competitions play the work as the composer published it almost ninety years ago. . . .

It was almost a century before the extraordinarily revealing original text of the Paganini Caprices was at last, in 1946, published from the manuscript in the possession of G. Ricordi & Co. in Milan (edited by M. Abbado and published by Suvini-Zerboni, Milan). It is only now that we see how the many accretions and simplifications have falsified the picture we had of these masterpieces of instrumental ingenuity. A single example will suffice; the Caprice No. 9 ('La Chasse') will corroborate what I have been writing in these pages about a regression in our use of the bow. In spite of Paganini's explicit instructions *sulla tastiera imitando il flauto* and *sulle terza e quarta corda, imitando il corno,* which presupposes the bow alternation ⊓ V and longish strokes, we nowadays only hear it with the monotonous

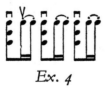 bowing, that the most widely used editions of the last decades have popularized. Gone is any attempt to imitate flutes or horns. Gone the evocation of a scene that the composer has sketched with such a sure hand and that tempted a Liszt, a Szymanowski, a Milhaud decades later.

But it is still more of a revelation when we see that the composer notated the E minor chord section with the bowing shown below demanding a truly Paganiniesque virtuosity of the right arm and obtaining the variety that only alternation of downbow and upbow chords can give. None of the currently available editions has gone as far in its demands as Paganini! They are all satisfied with the 'workaday' solution of

Ex. 4

with its unavoidable monotony. Paganini's original is:

Ex. 5

and the difficulty of alternating downbow and upbow chords, using the (presumably bouncing) bow at the lower half for the two semiquavers that precede each chord and keeping downbow and upbow indistinguishable in weight and quality, will prove an eye-opener. The labour-saving device advocated by all the editors follows the line of least resistance; but it is only by following what Artur Schnabel used to call the line of *most* resistance that the true effect can be achieved. This vital point was always a favourite of Schnabel's; and in 1940 he gave a series of lectures at Chicago University which were later published by the Princeton University Press, 1942, with the title *Music and the Line of Most Resistance.* The same contempt for short cuts and the line of least resistance in painting was shown by Whistler when he told the students at the Académie Carmen in Paris, where he taught for a couple of years towards the end of his life, 'I will show you the easiest way of getting into difficulties.'

Another similar feature of the Paganini manuscript is that the *saltando* episode is marked *alternating* downbow and upbow and not, as in current editions, each group of demisemiquavers downbow, each quaver upbow:

Ex. 6

We again see the importance that used to be accorded to alternating bowings. Fortunately the old Paganini edition by Edmund Singer (probably dating from 1880) which I used as a boy did not suppress (or rather censure) the original bowing and it gave me a choice of both. Thus I played it throughout my career (and recorded it too) with the original alternating *saltando*:

Ex. 7

Much of this reluctance to alternate seems due to a distrust of the bow-arm's ability to cope with chords of three notes both upbow and downbow and link these with an apparent legato. Ysaÿe played those impressive B major chorale-like chords in the second movement of Schumann's Second Sonata Op. 121 (Schumann gave it the title: *Zweite grosse Sonate*—and rightly so) with alternating up- and downbows, no gaps in between, resembling an organ. A few decades later an editor, who obviously had never played this Sonata in public, went out of his way to mark these chords to be played with successive downbows. This means inevitable gaps which destroy the chorale character so superbly realized by Ysaÿe. (The original Breitkopf edition does not contain bowing marks at this place, as the meaning is so explicit as to make any marking superfluous.)

Chord playing is generally plagued by superstitions: that chords have to be downbow always, that four-part chords have to be divided into two equal halves, that even *piano*—as at the end of the first movement of the Beethoven Sonata in A minor (Op. 23) or in the fourth variation of the Sonata Op. 30, No. 1—the chords cannot be taken upbow, lightly.

It is instructive to look at Paganini's autograph of the chord variation of the Caprice No. 24 and the Introduction of Caprice 11, where his notation is symbolic (like Bach's, Pisendel's and other masters) and not realistic, as in our editions:

Caprice 24   Caprice 11

Ex. 8

He writes just as symbolically as Bartók does in the Solo Sonata at bar 99 and in several other places, and as Bach very often does. (How could it be otherwise, for instance in the first bar of the Partita in B minor?)

Here is still another symbolic notation: from Ravel's *Tzigane* between 2 and 3 in the Cadenza:

Ex. 9

which I call symbolic in spite of the fact that a contortion of the hand does enable one to play it simultaneously. (D sharp with the first, B with the third and F with the second finger.)

A good way to persuade our right arm and our bow to be more daring in chord playing is by giving them the test of that chord passage in the Fourth (D minor) Concerto by Vieuxtemps which Bartók probably remembered when he wrote in the Cadenza of his Second Concerto:

Ex. 10

We are so poor in documentary evidence about performance tradition of a century ago, that at the risk of repeating myself, I will say that scraps of information (like Sir George Henschel's about Sarasate) or comparisons like these which I have just made between an earlier and a later edition of the Paganini Caprice are of great value to us and deserve the space we devote to what may seem to some minutiae.

How soon performance tradition vanishes was brought home to me when a pupil recently asked me to help him prepare for one of the competitions Wieniawski's D major Polonaise, which I had not played for over fifty years. Ysaÿe considered the fabulous virtuoso Wieniawski (1835–80) the greatest of his contemporaries. I had studied it with Hubay, who became Wieniawski's successor at the Brussels Conservatoire in 1882 (at the age of twenty-three). I found the music, the first unedited printing published by E. Girod, Paris, and to my joy recognized Hubay's pencil marks and small changes in my copy and, what is more, re-lived the sound, the panache, the typically nineteenth-century climate of Hubay's playing, as I tried to give my pupil the feel of this Polonaise, which is much more than a period piece.

What prompts these lines mainly is the constant revelation of how little one can depend on *Urtexts* without oral tradition supplementing it.

Ex. 11

became—*saltando* under Hubay's bow, often became , the

risoluto B minor passage was changed by Hubay from to and

so on. Although Wieniawski's junior by twenty-three years, Hubay must have heard him play it several times, so the profuse markings with which this (in former days famous) Polonaise abounds, had a different 'density' for him than for us to whom this style has become something so remote.

Maestoso, largamento, grazioso, risoluto, con fuoco and even *grandioso* and *furioso* are some of the recurring performance requirements of Wieniawski. Even if only considered as a corrective to our present non-*grandioso* and non-*furioso* and even non-*maestoso* playing style, pieces like his two Concertos and two Polonaises should be more used in the classroom than they are. This applies to Vieuxtemps' Concertos, too, some of whose performance requirements are an eye-opener to one accustomed to our young violinists, with their urbane smooth style which has no doubt been conditioned and moulded by respect, not to say fear, of the microphone and the monitor in the recording booth. In Vieuxtemps we find markings like *attacca con molto forza, vigoroso, leggierissimo, giocoso, brillante* and even *attacca con furia!*

Pianists are more history-conscious than we violinists are. They have their Alkans, Gottschalks, sometimes they even play post-Mendelssohnian Litolff.

CHAPTER 33

DISCUSSES CLOCKWISE AND COUNTER-CLOCKWISE
bowing and touches upon those other inexhaustible subjects:
bow articulation and fingerings

LET ME now go into a problem that most of us solve instinctively, but one that deserves to be put into words and thus made conscious. This is the use of fingerings that allow us to make *clockwise* bow movements, that is, from left to right, especially in fast *détaché* or *spiccato* figurations, instead of the other way around, which is, needless to say, always more difficult. An example from the Mozart Sonata K. 526 (first movement) will serve as an illustration. If we play

Ex. 1

with the traditional upper (third position) fingering, we will have to cope with two counter-clockwise movements (from A to G sharp and from D to C sharp). If we play it with my fourth position fingering, or even in the second position, the bow changes will come clockwise, and the fourth position will have the added advantage of bringing the F sharp

Ex. 2

within an easy stretch. And still even the most recent edition (1956) persists in the belief that the third position is the 'natural' choice!

It might seem obvious that in choosing our fingerings for fast *détaché* or *spiccato* figurations we should keep the comfort of the bow-arm in mind, yet this is ignored by editors. For instance, neither the Joachim nor the Flesch edition gives the fingering that would avoid the counter-clockwise bow movement in the Finale of the Mendelssohn Concerto:

Ex. 3

Yes, we violinists are a curious breed! We practise Paganini's Caprice No. 1 in *arpeggios*:

Ex. 4

but when I suggest some colleague should play, in the Mendelssohn Concerto *Finale*:

Ex. 5

instead of the usual fingering, he looks at me askance. . . . This passage too:

205

Ex. 6

is made easier with the lower fingering. Current editions—as far as I know—fail to give students food for thought, by urging them at least to experiment with both fingerings before deciding on the obvious one. In the Mozart–Kreisler *Rondo* the avoidance of the open strings in

Ex. 7

will probably come to most players instinctively, if they play it *spiccato*. (If played '*à la corde*' both fingerings are valid.) But they may not be aware that the second bar of this piece can be made easier both for bowing and for intonation, by playing it in the second position:

Ex. 8

Of course the two semitone shifts need a certain skill and the return from second to first position by the unorthodox means of

Ex. 9

will seem to some teachers questionable.

Conservative teachers will also look askance at my suggestion of playing

Ex. 10

in the last movement of the Beethoven Concerto, instead of the usual (upper) fingering. This obviously does not mean that we should (or that we can) avoid all counter-clock-wise bowing at all costs.

In the Presto of the G minor Sonata by Bach (for instance in the first bar) counter-clockwise bowings are inevitable, although it is conceivable to start it in the second position, thus:

Ex. 11

The Prelude of the E major Solo Partita offers a neat example in the *bariolage* section of both kinds, in succession, making a 'figure of eight' pattern.

It is difficult to understand why it is that practically all editors have failed to notate the following sequence in the Bach G minor Fugue with the only bowing that truly conforms to both the spirit and the letter of the text, that is by *starting upbow* and keeping this up throughout the passage.

Ex. 12

Not only does this do away with the clumsy

Ex. 13

but it avoids the musically redundant, and in downbow bowing inevitable, overemphasis of the D bass, which needs to be underplayed, if anything. This is assured by the ⌄⌄⌄ ⌄⌄⌄ bowing. (It goes without saying that the player must cultivate a light downstroke and in general find a judicious balance between a somewhat 'weighted' upbow and a correspondingly lighter-textured downbow.) And still editors have consistently evaded this logical solution, from F. David onwards to C. Flesch, and have suggested bowings

such as  or   or   or

hypnotized as they all seemed to be by the superstition that 'strong beat means downbow'! Once we are alerted to the existence of passages made unnecessarily difficult, we will find many that can be facilitated. Thus the following passage from the Bach Sonata in E for Violin and Clavier (second movement).

Ex. 14

Although we know that in runs that move from the E string downward the logical bow movement, that is, the slight raising of arm and elbow, comes easier on upbow than on downbow, we find the following in current editions of the Paganini Caprice No. 17:

Ex. 15

I suggest that students experiment with upbow on all but the one *upward run* which, by the same token, comes more naturally on the downbow (the one in B flat major).

Our respect for the printed page makes us accept many an uncomfortable and illogical bowing or fingering and prevents us from searching and experimenting. Take the familiar figure

Ex. 16

from the Mendelssohn Finale that we all play with the descending fragment

Ex. 17

upbow and in the first position in spite of the obviously somewhat awkward bow movement from A to D string. I was no exception and never
gave it a thought until just lately I realized—'after the event' as it were!—
that playing it in the second position makes it considerably easier. (In the
first case two notes on the A string, in the latter case two on the D string.)
Students of today (and tomorrow) will smile when they read that in the
original Breitkopf orchestral score (published presumably almost a hundred
years ago: Mendelssohn's *Werke*, Serie 4, No. 18) the editor—probably
F. David—took the trouble to finger this passage in an otherwise sparsely
fingered orchestral score in the 'up and down jumping' manner shown
below in order to avoid the stretch from C sharp to F sharp!

Ex. 18

As we have already given so much space to this supposedly unproblem-
atic passage, let us go one step further and see how it got gradually
simplified from F. David onwards.

Ex. 19

Flesch did away with Hubay's first finger slides (C sharp B, A sharp B) and
the one at the end of the second bar. I tried to make the bowing easier, and

209

used the half position in the second bar. Joachim's edition (1905) has the same slide of a third as Hubay's but at least shows us the way by combining the two 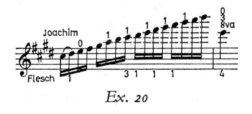 segments on a downbow in the second half of the first bar. That this results in the unrealistic demand of playing the whole second bar plus upbeat and the C sharp on one upbow shows that even great masters like Joachim, at the twilight of a glorious career, sometimes leave editorial duties to assistants. The Joachim fingering of the E major scale shortly before the coda of the Finale belongs here; Flesch tried to improve on these five successive shifts on first and second finger, but there are certainly still other possibilities open to us:

Ex. 20

To improve on given fingerings and bowings is more often possible than we think. In the C minor fingered octave section of the Paganini Caprice No. 17, I find it advisable to avoid the downbow in the third bar, especially as the  stresses are so constant in the whole section. This has other advantages too: it allows the upbeat to be taken upbow, and avoids over-emphasis on the four consecutive G's.

Ex. 21

It somehow lightens the texture of the whole strenuous technical 'feat'!
The 1964 Soviet Tchaikovsky Album is for the most part efficiently

edited but I find that the scale towards the end of Valse Scherzo Op. 34 is smoother with my (lower) fingering.

Ex. 22

I thought it worthwhile to devote space to these examples because of their heartening implication that things do change.

CHAPTER 34

SPECULATES UPON THE DECLINE
in the use by teachers and students of variations such as
those of Tartini and Paganini, written with a didactic aim.
Concludes that they cannot be safely dispensed with

IT IS A curious fact that those variation works which treat technical problems from many angles, and aim at a certain comprehensiveness, are on the way out (from the point of view of publishers and teachers between whom there undoubtedly exists a certain interdependence).

In saying this I am thinking principally of sets of Variations like the one that Tartini wrote on a Corelli theme (fifty variations entitled *l'Arte dell'Arco*) and Paganini's sixty on the 'Barucaba' theme (Op. 14) which were obviously written with a pedagogical intent and must have been widely used as a compact manual in their time. Nowadays publishers seem to favour specialized publications that hand out their wisdom in small doses that are, in fact, 'digests' instead of brave attempts like Tartini's and Paganini's.

In my own necessarily limited library there are only two recent editions of the Tartini: the Schirmer one of 1909 (probably out of print) and the Bulgarian State publication of 1964; as to the Paganini, only one practical edition came to my notice, the one published by Omega Music Edition, New York in 1951. In a previous book of mine* I pointed out the regrettable fact that only one of Tartini's fifty variations can be said to have come down to us: in the Kreisler *encore* number (Tartini–Kreisler Variations); the two other variations are Kreisler's invention.

* A Violinist's Notebook (*Gerald Duckworth, London 1964*).

These fifty variations have been aptly called an 'encyclopedia of eighteenth century bowing technique' and have been re-edited by illustrious pedagogues like Cartier, Léonard, and Ferdinand David. (Even cellists are benefiting from this compendium of bowing prowess since the famous French cellist Paul Bazelaire transcribed it for his instrument.)

Tartini's challenges are not solely directed to the bow-arm. Trills, grace notes, mordents abound, chords and double stoppings are combined with specifically right-arm problems and, what is perhaps most important, articulation seems to be an ever-present requirement in these variations.

The syncopated figures are often reinforced by *sforzandi* (Nos. 3, 12, 26, 30), the slight lifting of the bow between segments repeated on one stroke in No. 10 (and also 15)

Ex. 1

is given its due, as is also the graceful lifting towards the tip of the bow in No. 8

Ex. 2

(The student who may have thought that I am harping too much in my book on matters of articulation and of bow-lifting should note these written-out rests!)

What will come as a surprise to today's students is the presence of treasurable 'Tartinian' *cantabile* interludes between all these bow-technical variations in *spiccato* (demisemiquavers) in *con fuoco* mood, in flying *staccato* and so on. These *cantabile* variations exemplify the oft-quoted rule of the great Paduan: 'To play well, you must sing well.'

As for the Paganini, it is difficult to understand how a work of such inventiveness and usefulness could pass out of circulation. With all due respect to the wealth of classroom material we have at our disposal, I feel that we should not ignore a work which in its 'time-saving' modernity (sixteen bars per variation), the enormous range of its challenges and its shrewd pedagogical planning (every variation in a different key: eight in B major, four in F sharp, three in A flat and so on) stands alone in didactic literature. Written only five years before his death and dedicated to his friend Germi, a lawyer in Genoa, these variations were obviously meant to be a repository of the basic elements of the Paganinian technique rather than a challenge to rivals—of his own and of future time.

If we follow the implications of his text and establish our fingerings with the fabulous suppleness and stretching capacity of Paganini's hand in mind, we will find that a great deal in our contemporary fingering habits has been pre-figured by him.

In this work too we encounter much that is unexpected, as we do in the Tartini set: for instance, the *cantabile* variation in A flat (on the D string, No. 10), the one (No. 31) that demands great steadiness of the bow-arm, the tune being on the A string while the open E string drone has to be sustained (a much more demanding task than that in the D major Caprice No. 20, where the drone is on the D string and the tune on the A).

These remarks apply equally to No. 37 (of the Variations) with its A string drone alternating with an E string drone, while the figuration moves from E string to D string, ending in an A major scale:

Ex. 3

It is up to the vigilance of the student to take full advantage of what the Variations have to offer: to cite just a few examples: play '*due corde*' those scales in spread-out thirds* in No. 36; recognize those passages that were

* *By spread-out thirds I mean* 'abwechselnde Terzen'.

meant to be played in the fourth position (most of No. 18) and act accordingly; play the demisemiquaver segments of No. 7 with alternating up and down bow '*saltato*' as in the E major Caprice No. 9 ('*La Chasse*'), although these are marked *legato*, and in general spot those places where fingered octaves or *bariolage* are implied (though not specified in available editions). For instance in No. 7 where *bariolage* is meant, and certainly not third position with a stretched B on the A string.

Ex. 4

All this causes me to reflect upon the curious way in which young violinists keep on attempting short cuts: taking the plunge of the Bartók Solo Sonata before having passed through the Violin Duos (see Chapter 36), attempting the Bach Solo Sonatas before having used as stepping stones the violin transcriptions of the Cello Suites; attacking the Paganini Caprices without having taken advantage of the sixty Barucaba variations.

CHAPTER 35

IN THE MAIN A PLEA FOR THE USE
of that violinists' treasury, Bartók's forty-four Violin
Duets, incidentally discussing the ever-present matter of
articulation in fragments in the Bartók Second Concerto,
in Mendelssohn, Weber, Prokofiev, Bach, the 'Eroica' and
Brahms

WHEN SOME of Bela Bartók's forty-four Violin Duets were first presented in public, early in the 1930s, he prefaced them with the following words, which I would like to call 'the musical understatement of the first half of our century': 'These forty-four Duos for two violins were written with the same aim in mind, as formerly the (piano) series entitled "For Children". They aim at providing the pupils in the first few years of their studies, with performance pieces which possess the unadorned simplicity of old folk-music, with all its melodic and rhythmic particularities.'

These two slim volumes (forty-six pages) are filled with music that makes them a treasury for those who seek an entrance into Bartók's world; these Duos have now been recognized as of a stature (in spite of the miniature size of its units: 40 to about 90 seconds each) that makes a group of these worthy of inclusion in a programme of Bartók Quartets, which is saying a good deal.

But what concerns us here is not so much their proven eligibility for public performance as their enormous pedagogical value which has not yet been fully recognized by teachers.

For the purposes of this book, it seems to me more important to stress the benefits that the student can reap from familiarity with and substantial use of these Bartók Duos in practising, than to point out their many beauties; and to draw attention to those characteristics which will prove to be a key to the Rhapsodies, the Concerto, the two Sonatas of 1921, the Rumanian and Hungarian Dances and folk-tunes. (Unfortunately, in this respect too, students proceed the other way round: they tackle those works that are 'useful' to them on the platform or in broadcasting studios, before having acquired what Busoni called 'the key' to a new idiom.) I will, therefore, not try to classify these gems according to their use of the different modes, Dorian, Lydian and others, or point out the compositional prowess that has gone into their making. I will rather draw attention to the practical benefits that this 'High School' in bow articulation, in the realization of a declamatory or *parlando* line, of accentuating cross rhythms, that at first seem to 'go against the grain' but turn out to be perfectly convincing, and point out the benefits they will bring to the student who takes them up in the spirit in which Bartók sent them out into the world.

Bow articulation, the use of the lower part of the bow, of minute stoppings on the strings, or of minute liftings off the strings, which—alas—our present playing style avoids (several critical voices have been heard about this recently) can and will be benefited by these technically deceptively simple pieces, precisely because their very essence 'forbids' anything less than natural articulation and bow phrasing. This may sound far-fetched, but I think any teacher can prove this to his own satisfaction by testing some pupil who is particularly recalcitrant to sense-making phrasing, to the stopping, lifting of the bow, etc. He will find, that whereas in some repertoire piece by one of the masters this pupil is inclined to

disregard the articulation implicit in ♪♪♪♪ or ♪ ♪♪ ♪ ♪ or ♪♪♪♪♪♪♪

and to distort these by a smooth gapless bowing style, probably in the upper portion of the bow, he will be unable to play havoc with Bartók's phrases, since these are so explicitly *dependent* upon just the right use of the bow that he obviously had in mind. When Bartók writes in No. 29 (New Year's Song No. 2)

Ex. 1

and puts a dot on each of the  motifs (something that the masters neglected to do, for the good reason that in former times *every* player con-
sidered this self-evident, and therefore executed it correctly by instinct)
even the unmusical pupil will by the nature of the phrase be impelled to
apply a minute lifting of the bow. The same goes for the second violin
part of No. 34 (Counting Song):

Ex. 2

or for the Ruthenian Dance (No. 35), where neither the cross-accented
accompaniment

Ex. 3

nor the tune

Ex. 4

can be played in any other bowing manner than at the nut and well articulated. In the same way the contrast between the playing procedure of the
drone in the second violin part of No. 36 (the bag-pipe) and the tune in the
first part is so unmistakable:

Ex. 5

unarticulated 'non-stop' bowing for the drone and sharply articulated playing with minute stopping between the phrases involving the figure ♪♪♩ that even the least gifted pupil will familiarize himself with the contrasting procedures. I assume of course that the player will always study both parts and alternate with his partner; and practising one of the parts while reading and *imagining* the other one will be an invaluable lesson at this elementary stage of score-reading. The accents and – signs in No. 38 (Rumanian Whirling Dance) make the bowing procedure just as unmistakable as if the ♪♪♩ ♪♪♩ ♪♪♩ had been marked with a dot on each repeated fragment and the – sign had been provided with an additional dot on the crotchets ♩ .

It may seem to the casual reader that I am harping too much on this question of articulation, lifting of the bow at the end of ♪♪♩ motifs and the like. But the fact that Bartók went to the trouble of providing each of these forty-seven figures with a dot in the sixth variation of the second movement of the Second Violin Concerto (bars 83 to 104) surely shows how conscious he was that the right characterization of this 'Scherzo variation' is entirely dependent upon just this quality of articulated bowing. Bartók was not 'trusting', as Mendelssohn when he sent out into the world the Finale of the Violin Concerto or the Scherzo of the D minor Trio was 'trusting' to the sense of style and the tradition-consciousness of the violinists of the mid-nineteenth century, who did *not* need to be told that motifs in such context meant infinitesimal liftings of the bow and slight inflections on the first of the semiquavers. Joachim, who had often played it under the composer's direction, was no longer as 'trusting' as Mendelssohn was: in 1905, when he edited it for the Joachim–Moser *Violinschule*, he did mark the ♪♪♩ with dots under the slurs.

And do we not still today sometimes hear this matchless Mendelssohn Finale misrepresented something like this?

Ex. 6

No pianist who plays Weber's *Rondo brilliant* (Op. 62) (and no violinist who tackles it in Max Rostal's transcription) would dare to commit such an articulation misdemeanour.

Ex. 7

One of the most played Sonatas of our time, the D major by Prokofiev Op. 94, owes a good deal of its popularity to the irresistible brilliance of its Scherzo, that depends on the same controlled bow stopping and sharp articulation as the Mendelssohn Finale and the Bartók Variation.

Composers of our time are less trusting than their elders were: Prokofiev makes sure of the right bow lifting by notating the tune in the slow movement of his Second Concerto with an unmistakable semiquaver rest:

Ex. 8

This rest is in fact exactly what I have described earlier in these pages as a *'reprise de l'archet'* (re-taking of the bow). Only in former times it used not to be written out! Earlier in the slow movement of the Second Prokofiev Concerto (nineteen bars from the beginning) we find six cesuras in four bars, which in former times would not have been notated, but would have been understood as a matter of course and played accordingly. In the four bars that follow the cesuras, we again find them, made foolproof by the notation:

Ex. 9

Such precautions were not necessary in Mozart's time, when professional instrumentalists phrased and articulated as naturally as they breathed. Wanda Landowska, quoting those 'who had the good fortune to hear Mozart play the pianoforte' speaks of it as 'punctated by *interrogation and exclamation marks, and by cesuras*' (the italics are mine). One has to admit that editions of certain masterpieces are becoming more outspoken, more explicit in recent years.

An editor like Max Schneider does not hesitate to demand of the violinist who partners the oboe in Bach's Concerto for Violin and Oboe (Breitkopf, 1949) three consecutive downbows in the last movement on

Ex. 10

This ensures an equality of impact on the three G's that could not be achieved in any other way. Just as in the Beethoven 'Eroica' conductors nowadays often direct violinists to bow this passage with consecutive downbows:

Ex. 11

To return to Bartók. The exemplary concordance between his intention and his markings is particularly striking in the Tempo I of No. 40 (Walachian Dance)

Ex. *12*

where one might say he makes the cesura 'foolproof' by writing out the
semiquaver rests, and 'composes' the cesura at the end of each of these four
bars by making the Dance a $\frac{5}{4}$ one instead of the $\frac{4}{4}$ tempo of the Exposition.
It is not only by scrupulously exact notation and metronome markings but
also by indicating the duration of each piece (43 seconds or 38 seconds or
2 minutes and 6 seconds for example) that he tries to insure the pieces
against distortion through arbitrary tempi and through 'interpretation'
generally as we see it applied to masterpieces. . . . (Do we not read any day
in reviews of recordings that X's performance of Beethoven's B flat Piano
Concerto is 'a full four minutes faster' than the one by Y ?)

I am stressing all this in support of my contention that the unmistakable
character of the very essence of these folk-based pieces and the exactitude of
their notation makes them pedagogically invaluable and will provide the
pupil in an indirect manner with violinistic know-how that Etudes written
with a professedly pedagogical intent sometimes fail to give him.

It is self-evident that the differences in tempo of playful pieces of the $\frac{2}{4}$
basic pattern will force the student to differentiate in bow-speed, bouncing
procedure, bow pressure, etc., when No. 26 is marked $\frac{2}{4}$ *Scherzando, piano,
leggero* ♩=116; No. 27 *Allegro non troppo, forte* ♩=126; No. 32 *Allegro
giocoso*, $\frac{4}{4}$, *forte* ♩=132; No. 36 *Allegro molto*, $\frac{2}{4}$ *forte* ♩=152–156; No. 9
Allegro non troppo, $\frac{2}{4}$ *forte* ♩=120; No. 22, *Allegro molto pianissimo*, $\frac{2}{4}$ ♩=184.
The inherent logic and the concordance between musical content and
playing procedure cannot fail to reveal itself even to 'the pupils in the first
few years of their studies'—as Bartók expressed himself in his prefatory
remarks.

And this naturally goes for the other groups of pieces too. The poignant
beauty of No. 28 ('Sadness'), of the bitonal No. 11 ('Cradle Song'), of No. 23

(*Lento rubato*) ('Song of the Bride'), with their '*parlando*' eloquence will spur the beginner (and the accomplished virtuoso too), to efforts in the differentiated application of *vibrato,* bow articulation, pressure, and bow-speed, which are the very essence of these pieces. The serene lyricism of Nos. 10, 12, 19 (in $3 + \frac{3}{8} + 2$ time, which is something very different from $\frac{4}{4}$ time, in Bartók's language!) and of No. 21 is worlds apart from the earthy, weighty *élan* of No. 44 (*Allegro moderato* ♩= 84), of the two Hungarian Marches (Nos. 17 and 18), the New Year's Song No. 4 (No. 31) (mostly in $\frac{5}{8}$ time alternating with bars in $\frac{3}{8}$) with its diction that gives the impression that one is hearing the words and syllables of the text. No. 33 ('Song of the Harvest') also belongs to this type.

Some of the pieces seem to have been written with a definite pedagogical aim, so the lilting Burlesque (No. 16) where even the most recalcitrant

bow-arm will be compelled to respect the phrasing  and the *Scherzo* (No. 41)

Vivace ♩ = 140–160

Ex. 13

that begins in deceptive simplicity only to trip up the players and test their presence of mind with disjointed thematic fragments tossed from one player to the other, with interjected *pizzicato* accompaniments, canonic playfulness, augmentations through inserted silent beats. But I think that the 'Serbian Dance' (No. 39) is the supreme test piece of this collection from the point of view of muscle control and coordination; one could call the way the *sforzandi* fight each other in the two competing violins a sort of counterpoint of rhythmic *élan*. One is tempted to put down here the whole of these last sixteen bars; and one is also tempted to attribute the reluctance of some teachers to use this work as a whole to their unwillingness to face challenges like these sixteen bars in front of their pupils. . . . I have no means of ascertaining whether piano teachers have carried out their duty towards their pupils more conscientiously in utilizing the treasures of *Mikrokosmos* than their violin colleagues have done with respect to the forty-four Violin Duos, but it seems to me that they have.

It is not only in passages of gossamer lightness like those I have just recalled that an unmistakable notation has become desirable, not to say necessary, in our days when players have accustomed listeners to a less sophisticated use of the bow. It is also most useful in comparatively tranquil passages like bar 262 in the third movement of Bartók's Second Violin Concerto, where the composer makes sure by his notation that the intended articulation will not be betrayed by the performer.

Ex. 14

Observe how he differentiates between a ‿ and a dot coming at the end of a *legato* fragment! We who use editions that go back seventy or eighty years and—side by side with them—contemporary works edited with the care and sophistication to which Gustav Mahler, Richard Strauss, and Debussy have accustomed us, sometimes forget that we have to use our imagination in those older unedited scores where guideposts like Bartók's are missing. What even the average player of Mozart's or Haydn's time executed instinctively has to be made unequivocally clear to Stravinsky's or Bartók's contemporaries, either by the composer or by his editor. To mention just one instance: the sign ‿ (longish stroke with stopping of the bow at the end) was, as far as I know, not used before about 1910.

This is the reason why Brahms, when he published that elusive scherzo-like third movement in a minor key in his Op. 108 Violin Sonata, did not make it clear that he expected the violinist to use a *parlando* articulation on each of the ♩♩ or ♪♩♩ motifs by notating them ♩♩ or ♪♩♩. He did express his wish unequivocally by giving it the heading: *un poco presto e con sentimento,* and by the very texture of the movement and of its interchanges between the essentially percussive instrument and the bowed, lyrical one. Those violinists with whom Brahms must have played it—Joachim, Hubay and perhaps others—certainly understood '*à demi mot*' what his intention was: that the violin's quavers should have something of the articulateness of stammered, whispered words of two and three syllables, and that the piano should try to rival the expressiveness of the violin and give up some of the *staccato*-dryness inherent in any keyboard instrument. Disregard of the *un poco presto*, so frequent nowadays, and the *à la corde* playing (in too fast a *tempo*) of this lovely piece, robs it of the *con sentimento* that Brahms demanded, and thus we can sometimes experience an otherwise brilliant performance of a piece whose character and climate have been entirely changed on account of tempo, bowing, touch, pedalling and similar elusive factors.

CHAPTER 36

CONCLUSION

JUST BEFORE reaching the end of these pages, I have been looking through some volumes on technique sent to me over the last forty or forty-five years by hopeful publishers or authors. I have not used them or looked into them for decades—until now. How hopefully their authors must have gone through the tremendous labour of compiling, making a fair copy, proof-reading, promoting them among colleagues and conservatoires and how comparatively sterile all these efforts have proved to be! And the efforts of those students who worked at them day after day, month after month, for hours at a time. . . .

There is one volume of over 200 large pages of twelve or thirteen lines of exercises on each, some of these probably quite useful (for the right student at the right moment). Two thousand five hundred lines of exercises by a concert violinist and pedagogue, whose name used to be quite familiar to me. Exercises that probably 'cover' innumerable difficulties, hazards, eventualities, into the compilation of which went much thought, foresight, the desire to help.

But as I look at it now, I see behind it all an almost pathological hoarding instinct (perhaps my own book is not quite exempt from this instinct?) and besides: a typically Germanic urge for 'completeness' which they call '*Restlosigkeit*'. (My own book at least is not guilty of *this*.)

Then I look at another volume: a sumptuously produced one of 260 pages, claiming to be the 'royal road' to violin mastery, based on what the author calls technical analysis; a book weighing two and a half pounds. With it goes a violin part of the Beethoven Violin Concerto, technically 'analysed' on forty-nine pages, mostly four lines to a page, the rest of it taken up by minutely detailed instructions to the student. Such volumes obviously proceed from the idea that technique on the one hand, musician-ship, sense of style and the other musical virtues on the other hand are

226

objectives that can be tackled separately, each in its own good time. This fallacy is hardly to be wondered at when one of our most successful violinists in a recent interview delivered himself of the statement that it was a mistaken notion that violin playing was difficult. He himself had all the technique in the world by the time he had reached the age of seven. But (he went on to say) the rest of his life had to be spent conquering the purely musical values, and so on and so forth.

This is typical of the outlook that I have been trying to combat both in my teaching and in my writings, the outlook which assumes that after having disposed of the technical chores one can concentrate on these musical objectives in neat succession.

Whether I have been successful in conveying my thoughts about these questions in these present pages is not for me to judge. No wonder that melancholy thoughts take hold of one at the moment of finishing a book. But a consoling glimpse helps me: even if these pages eventually go 'the way of all books', the student who picks up an unopened, unused copy a couple of decades hence, in some second-hand bookshop, need not pity the author. While gathering these materials, my labours have not been sordidly mechanistic like the work which went into those manuals. While working on it I have been constantly in the presence of Music.

INDEX

NOTE: All works mentioned are those for the violin, unless otherwise indicated

Abbado, M., 199
Art du Violon, L,' (Cartier), 138, 140
Art of Violin Playing (Flesch), 20, 33–4, 115, 169
Arte dell' Arco Variations (Tartini), 136, 212–13, 214
Auer, Leopold, 19, 73; his playing, 171–2; his school, 3, 4*n*, 171–2; and Tchaikovsky Concerto, 198–9

Babitz, Sol, 115
Bach, J. S., 68–9; misprints in, 127–31; rhythmic distortions, 157–8
  A minor Adagio and Fugue, 11
  C major Adagio and Fugue, 11, 12
  Cantatas, 125
  Cello Suites, 18, 122, 215
  Brandenburg Concerto No. 4, 94
  Brandenburg Concerto No. 6, 107
  Chaconne, 4, 10, 11, 12, 74, 110, 111*n*, 121, 124, 125, 128–9, 137; bowing device, 178; divergent readings, 113–19; rhythmic distortions in, 157–8
  Double Concerto, 5
  E major Concerto, 182
  Concerto for Violin and Oboe, 221
  A minor Fugue, 103–8, 110–11, 112–13, 125, 181

  C major Fugue, 101–3, 125, 126, 176, 186
  G minor Fugue, 101, 108–10, 112, 125, 127–8, 207–8
  'Goldberg' Variations, 18
  B minor Partita (Sarabande), 115, 130
  D minor Partita, 98–100, 193
  E major Partita, 4, 10, 207
  E major Prelude, 4, 74, 124–5, 130, 170, 190
  Solo Sonatas and Partitas, 108, 110, 111, 123–6, 182, 215
  A minor Solo Sonata, 74, 120, 124, 125, 131, 161–2
  C major Solo Sonata, 186
  G minor Solo Sonata, 11, 12, 66, 120, 124, 125, 127, 161, 207
  Sonata No. 2 in A major for Violin and Clavier, 48, 49
  Sonata No. 3 for Violin and Clavier, 48, 59, 194, 208
  Sonata No. 4 in C minor for Violin and Clavier, 78
  Sonata No 6 in G major for Violin and Clavier, 179
Baillot, Pierre, 147
Bartók, Béla, 52, 68; and articulation, 217–19, 221–4; on competitions, 14; his pattern of fourths, 85–6

Bartók, Béla—*cont.*
  Second Concerto, 39, 64, 84, 85–6, 202;
    articulation, 219, 224
  String Quartets, 188
  String Quartet No. 4, 78, 188
  First Rhapsody, 50, 85, 86, 144, 185–6
  Second Rhapsody, 147
  First Sonata, 53, 84, 85
  Second Sonata, 12, 154
  Solo Sonata, 124, 201, 215
  Forty-four Violin Duets, 38, 186, 216–19,
    221–4
'Barucaba' Variations (Paganini), 212, 213–
  15
Bazelaire, Paul, 213
Beecham, Sir Thomas, 6, 8
Beethoven, Ludwig van, 11, 18, 52
  Concerto, 6–7, 8, 10, 22, 58, 84, 132, 207;
    Auer's playing of, 171; bowing
    problem, 195; his changes of mind
    in, 143–7; fingered octaves, 80–1;
    Joachim's playing of, 174, 175;
    Kreisler's cadenza, 95
  B flat Piano Concerto, 222
  C major Quartet, 10
  C sharp minor Quartet, 174
  Quartet Op. 127, 77
  Quartet Op. 132, 10
  Romances, 5, 12, 192; F major, 10; G
    major, 56
  A minor Sonata, 162, 201
  C minor Sonata, 5, 6, 11, 60, 147–8, 163
  D minor Sonata, 197, 224–5
  Sonata Op. 12, No. 1, 47–8
  Sonata Op. 12, No. 2, 166–7
  Sonata Op. 12, No. 3, 196
  Sonata Op. 30, No. 1, 132–3, 201
  Sonata Op. 30, No. 2, 60
  Sonata Op. 30, No. 3, 49, 52–3, 55, 59,
    195–6
  Sonata Op. 96, 131–2, 162–3
  Hammerklavier Sonata, 148
  'Kreutzer' Sonata, 4, 7, 10, 11, 12, 55,
    131, 162
  'Spring' Sonata, 5, 11, 12, 137
  Piano Sonata Op. 53, 163
  'Eroica' Symphony, 221
  Trio Op. 1, No. 3, 60
  Trio Op. 70, No. 1, 60
  Trio Op. 97, 163
Belgian School of String Playing, 173
Bendiner, Alfred, 30–1
Berceuse (Merkler), 3
Berg, Alban, 68
  Kammerkonzert, 144
Bériot, Charles de, 38, 173
Berufs-Krankheiten des Musikers (Flesch), 35
Biber, Heinrich von, 126
Bischoff, Dr Hans, 105
Bloch, Ernst, 11
  'Nigun', 180
Bogas, Roy, 68
Böhm, Joseph, 73
Boston Symphony Orchestra, 22, 171
Boyden, David D., 111, 115, 135
Brahms, Johannes: rhythmic and tempo
    distortion, 158–9, 163–5
  Concerto, 5, 7, 8, 63–4, 84, 91, 96, 164,
    165; bowing device, 178; Joachim's
    playing of, 174–5; tempo distor-
    tion, 164, 165
  Hungarian Dance, 10
  A major Sonata, 12
  D minor Sonata, 6, 8, 11, 12, 67, 197,
    224; distortion in, 158–9, 163–4
  G major Sonata, 12, 134, 164–5, 179
Breitkopf & Härtel, 140
Britten, Benjamin, 41
Brodsky, Adolf, 198
Brosa, Antonio, 41
Bruch, Max:
  Concerto, 4, 10, 61, 90–1, 92, 96
Brussels Conservatoire, 19, 202
Budapest Quartet, 11
Burmester, Willi, 125, 171
Busch, Adolf, 19, 100*n*, 101, 103, 113, 118,
    122, 124, 127, 129, 130, 136, 178
Busoni, Ferruccio, 6, 10, 19, 115, 121, 123,
    217
  Concerto, 8
  Second Sonata, 11

Calouste Gulbenkian Foundation, 25
Campagnoli, Bartolomeo, 38
Capet, Lucien, 20, 101, 103, 113, 117, 121,
    129

'Carnival of Venice' Variations (Haydn), 9
Cartier, Jean-Baptiste, 213; and Tartini sonatas, 138, 139
Casals, Pablo, 23, 122
Casella, Alfredo, 148
Celentano, John, 43
Champeil, J., 102, 110, 113, 114, 118, 121, 128
Chopin, Frédéric, 10, 12
Clement, Franz, 143
Cleveland Orchestra, 42
Cocteau, Jean, 170
Collegium Musicum, 23
Colonne Orchestra, 20
Confalonieri, Giulio 9
Corder, Frederick, 4
Corelli, Arcangelo: editors' liberties with, 137–8; Tartini variations on theme of, 212–13, 214
    La Follía, 5, 136, 179
    Sonata No. 1, Op. 5, 137
    Sonata No. 6, Op. 5, 111–12, 137–8
Cortot, Alfred, 27–8
Czerny, Carl, 146–7, 148

David, Ferdinand, 101, 103, 109, 113, 117, 123, 128, 129, 136, 141, 208, 209, 213
De Vito, Giaconda, 11
Debussy, Claude, 11; marking of glissandi, 150–2, 153
    Après-Midi d'un Faune, L', 144
    Fille aux Cheveux de Lin, La, 183
    'Minstrels', 153–4
    Sonata, 68, 150–2, 153
Deutsche Orchestervereinigung (1962), 22
Devil's Trill (Tartini), 5, 11, 12, 74–5, 136, 138–40
Dittersdorf, Carl Ditters von, 11
Doflein, Erich, 39; Method, 38–40
Dulow, G., 140
Duo Concertant (Stravinsky), 148
Dvořák, Antonin, 11

Einstein, Alfred, 135
Elgar, Sir Edward:
    Concerto, 8, 170
Elman, Mischa, 3, 5, 6, 124, 171, 172
Emily Anderson Award, 17

Enesco, Georges, 113, 141
Ernst, Heinrich, 73
    F sharp minor Concerto, 4

Fantasia (Gernsheim), 10
'Faust' Fantasy (Wieniawski), 3, 5
Fille aux Cheveux de Lin, La (Debussy), 183
Flesch, Carl, 11, 20, 32, 33–4, 35, 42, 81, 131, 170, 172; and Bach's Chaconne, 115, 117, 121; and Bach's Fugues, 98–100, 101, 102, 104, 109, 127, 208; and Beethoven's Concerto, 145–6; and Mendelssohn's Concerto, 81–3, 169, 209
Flesch, Dr Julius, 35
Follía, La (Corelli), 5, 136, 179
Fondazione Alberto Curci, 17
Fontaine d'Aréthuse (Szymanowski), 189
Ford Foundation, 24, 31
Forty-four Violin Duets (Bartók), 38, 186, 216–19, 221–4
Fournier, Pierre, 19
Franck, César:
    Sonata, 5, 12, 59, 144
Frankenstein, Alfred, 122
Franko, Sam, 174–5
French Ministry of Cultural Affairs, 25, 32

Geigenbüchlein (Kauder), 41
Geneva competition, 28
Geneva Conservatoire, 34, 89
Genoa competition, 28, 31
Genzmer, H., 38
Gernsheim, Friedrich, 10
Glazunoff, Alexander:
    Concerto, 191–2
'Goldberg' Variations (Bach), 18
Goldmark, Carl:
    Concerto, 4
Graded Course of Violin Playing (Auer), 172
Grieg, Edvard:
    C minor Sonata, 159–60
Grumiaux, Arthur, 11
Gulda, Friedrich, 13–14

Hallé, Lady (Wilma Neruda-Hallé), 175–6
Hambourg, Jan, 113, 114, 118

Handel, G. F., 175; editors' liberties with, 142
Sonata in A, 10
Sonata in D major, 12, 61, 142, 193
Hanslick, Eduard, 198
Harrison, May, 5
Harty, Sir Hamilton:
D minor Concerto, 6
Hauswald, Günter, 113
Haydn, Joseph, 9, 10, 11
Quartet Op. 33, No. 2, 155
Heifetz, Jascha, 3, 105, 112, 113, 118, 171, 172
Hellmesberger, J., 137; his edition of Bach, 102, 103, 104, 109, 110, 112, 113, 117, 120, 121, 123, 128, 129
Helsinki Conservatoire, 19
Henle, Dr G., 131, 134
Henschel, Sir George, 169–70, 171, 175
Hess, Dame Myra, 6
Hessen, State Music Library of, 149
Hindemith, Paul, 12, 38
Solo Sonatas, 78, 186–7
Studies for Violinists, 77–8
'Histoire d'un Soldat' Suite (Stravinsky), 144
History of Violin Playing (Boyden), 111, 115, 135
Hohe Schule des Violinspiels (David), 141
Hubay, Jeno, 19, 225; author's studies with, 3–5, 202–3; his edition of Bach, 101, 103, 109, 113, 114, 118, 121, 128; and Beethoven Concerto, 81, 143, 146; and Mendelssohn Concerto, 76, 209; and Tartini sonatas, 138, 141; and Wieniawski D major Polonaise, 202–3
Concerto all' Antica, 5
Concerto No. II, 5
Scène de la Csarda No. II, 5
Variations, 5
Huberman, Bronislav, 11, 198
Hungarian Concerto (Joachim), 10, 175
Hungarian Dances (Brahms), 10
'Hymn to the Emperor' (Haydn), 9

Joachim, Joseph, 9, 10, 19, 50, 61, 73, 86, 225; his playing, 174–6; and Bach Chaconne, 113, 114, 122; and Bach

Fugues, 101, 103, 113, 126, 127, 176; and Beethoven Concerto, 81, 143, 145, 146; and Mendelssohn Concerto, 82, 83, 210, 219; and Tartini sonatas, 138, 140
Hungarian Concerto, 10, 175

Kadosa, P., 38
Kammerkonzert (Berg), 144
Kauder, Hugo, 41
Kayser, H. E., 38, 39
Klemperer, Otto, 174
Kreisler, Fritz, 6, 8, 10, 11, 95, 124; his playing, 170–1, 182–3, 194; and Corelli sonatas, 137; and Tartini sonatas, 136, 138, 140
Kreisler (Pugnani): Allegro, 92, 136, 137
Kreutzer, Rodolphe:
Etudes, 7, 61, 63
Etudes-Caprices, 75–6
'Kreutzer' Sonata (Beethoven), 4, 7, 10, 11, 12, 55, 131, 162
Kubelik, Jan, 3, 124
Küchler, Ferdinand, 71–2
Kulenkampf, Georg, 19
Kulka, Konstantyn, 16
Kurth, Ernst, 128

Laló, Édouard, 11
Symphonie Espagnole, 49
Landowska, Wanda, 221
Lang, François, collection, 144
Lang, Paul Henry, 125
Leclair, Jean-Marie, 142n
Lemaitre, Paul, 113
Leningrad Conservatoire, 28
Léonard, H., 136, 141, 213
Leppard, Raymond, 119
Levin, Dr Julius, 176
Lindley, Robert, 173
Liszt, Franz, 10
Locatelli, Pietro, 11
Sonatas, 175

Marsick, Martin, 34
Marteau, Henri, 89, 124
Mattheson, Johann, 105

Mendelssohn, Felix, 11, 123, 175
  Concerto, 4, 10, 50–1, 59, 76, 81–3, 87,
    88, 92, 96, 168, 169; articulation, 219;
    bowing problem, 190, 191, 197;
    clockwise bowing, 205–6; 'enhance-
    ment', 188–9; fingerings, 208–10;
    Sarasate's playing of, 169, 175
  D minor Trio, 219
Mengelberg, Willem, 171
'Minstrels' (Debussy), 153–4
Monteverdi, Claudio, 188
Montreal competition, 29, 124
Moodie, Alma, 11
Moscow competition, 29
Moscow Conservatoire, 19
Moser, Andreas, 72–3, 122
Mostras, K., 110–11, 113, 119
Moto Perpetuo (Paganini), 10
Mozart, Leopold, 38, 40
Mozart, Wolfgang, 11, 18, 221
  A major Concerto, 5, 8, 49
  D major Concerto, 8, 40, 63, 86, 182–3,
    191
  G major Concerto, 89
  G minor Concerto, 8
  Piano Concertos, 126
  Quartet (K. 590), 83
  A major Sonata, K. 526, 54, 57; clock-
    wise bowing, 204–5
  Sonata K.378, 133
  Sonata K.454, 134
  Ten Celebrated Quartets (Einstein), 135
Mozart-Kreisler:
  Rondo, 54, 194, 206
Music and the Line of Most Resistance
  (Schnabel), 200
Music to My Eyes (Bendiner), 30–1
Musings and Memories of a Musician
  (Henschel), 169
My Life of Music (Wood), 175–6

Nachez, T., 138, 141
Nardini, Pietro, 11
National Council on the Arts (U.S.A.), 24
Neruda, Wilma (Lady Hallé), 175–6
Nether-Rhenish Music Festival (1877),
  169
Neuhaus, Heinrich, 27

New York Philharmonic Orchestra, 24
Nikisch, Artur, 6

Orff, Carl, 38
Ormandy, Eugène, 23

Paganini, Niccolo, 4, 9, 11, 36, 37, 170
  'Barucaba' Variations, 212, 213–15
  Caprices, 4, 8, 73, 93, 94, 133, 171, 190,
    193, 214, 215; bowing problem,
    199–200, 201, 205, 208; fingering,
    210
  D major Concerto, 49
  Moto Perpetuo, 10
Paris Conservatoire, 27, 28, 32
Parlow, Kathleen, 5, 171
Pasdeloup Orchestra, 20
Phantasie (Schumann), 10
Philadelphia Orchestra, 23
Pisendel, Johann Georg:
  Solo Sonata in A minor, 74, 126, 195
Pizzetti, Ildebrando, 11
Playford, J., 39
Portrait-Souvenir (Cocteau), 170
Prihoda, Vasa, 11
Prokofiev, Serge, 11, 12
  Concerto No. 1, 184–5
  Concerto No. 2, 78–9, 187, 220
  D major Sonata, 220
  F minor Sonata, 187–8
Pugnani, Gaetano (Kreisler), 92, 136, 137

Queen's Hall, 6

Ravel, Maurice:
  Sonata, 154, 155–6, 184
  Tzigane, 187, 202
Reger, Max, 11
Respighi, Ottorino, 136
  Sonata, 12
Ricordi, Tito, 9
Ries, F., 10, 147
Rondo Brillante (Weber), 220
Rondo Capriccioso (Saint-Saëns), 5, 10,
  160–1
Rostal, Max, 220
Rubinstein, Anton, 5, 11

St Francis Legend (Liszt), 10
'St Patrick's Day' (Haydn), 9
Saint-Saëns, Camille, 11
    Concerto, 4, 6, 10, 12, 182
    Rondo Capriccioso, 5, 10, 160–1
Sarasate, Pablo, 5, 10, 12, 124, 142*n*; his
    playing, 169–70, 175
Sauret, Émile, 10, 145, 146, 198
Scarlatti, Alessandro, 18
Schalk, Franz, 20
Schering, Arnold, 107
Schnabel, Artur, 19, 134, 200
Schneider, Max, 142, 221
Schneiderhan, Wolfgang, 19
Schonborn, Count, 23
Schubert, Franz, 12, 18
    Fantaisie Op. 159, 11
    Op. 162, 12
    A minor Sonatina, 87, 168
    D major Sonatina, 88
    G minor Sonatina, 53, 88
Schumann, Robert, 123, 131
    Phantasie, 10
    A minor Sonata, 10, 12, 131; neglect of,
      65–8
    D minor Sonata, 10, 11
    Toccata, 10
    Träumerei, 68
Schweitzer, Albert, 68–9, 125
Scriabin, A. H., 18
Seiber, Matyas, 38
Servais, A. F., 173
Sevčik method, 3, 79
Sgambati, Giovanni, 11
Shaw, George Bernard, 126, 176
Sibelius contest (Helsinki 1965), 44
Sinding, Christian, 4, 6, 11
Singer, Edmund, 73, 200
Sinigaglia, Leone, 11
Smetana, Bedřich, 11, 12
Società del Quartetto (Milan), 9–12
Spalding, Albert, 138
Spohr, Louis, 38
    Concerto VIII, 10, 62, 175
Stern, Isaac, 11
Stock Exchange Amateur Orchestral
    Society, 7

Stravinsky, Igor, 11
    Duo Concertant, 148
    '*Histoire d'un Soldat*' Suite, 144
Studies for Violinists (Hindemith), 77–8
Suk, Josef, 11
Svendsen, Johan, 11
Szell, George, 8, 42–3, 144, 195
Szymanowski, Karol, 11, 12
    Fontaine d'Arethuse, 189

Tanglewood (U.S.A.) String Symposium
    (1963, 1964), 22
Tartini, Giuseppe, 11, 175; editors' liber-
    ties with, 136, 138–42
    D minor Concerto, 141
    G minor Concerto, 10
    Devil's Trill, 5, 11, 12, 74–5, 136, 138–40
    A minor Sonata, 141
    G major Sonata, 141
    G minor Sonata (*Didone Abbandonata*),
      136, 178
    Arte dell' Arco Variations, 136, 212–13,
      214
Tartini-Léonard
    Sonata in G major, 93
Tchaikovsky, P. Ilyich:
    Concerto, 5, 12, 49, 95, 105, 181;
      bowing problem, 198–9
    Scherzo Op. 42, No. 2, 55
    Valse-Scherzo Op. 34, 95, 211
Tchaikovsky competition (Moscow 1966),
    23, 198
Ten Celebrated Quartets (Einstein), 135
Theme and Variations (Walter), 174
Thibaud, Jacques, 6, 20, 34, 124
Tomasini, L., 147
Träumerei (Schumann), 68
Tyson, Alan, 143–4, 147
Tzigane (Ravel), 187, 202

Valse Caprice (Wieniawski), 3
Valse Scherzo (Tchaikovsky), 95, 211
Vecsey, Franz von, 3, 5
Veracini, Francesco, 11
Vienna State Opera and Music Academy,
    20

Vieuxtemps, Henri, 4, 139, 140, 147, 203
  Ballade et Polonaise, 62
  A minor Concerto, 10
  D minor Concerto, 202
  E major Concerto, 3
  Etudes, 4
Violinist's Notebook, A (Szigeti), 212n
Viotti, Giovanni, 73
  A minor Concerto, 4, 11, 62–3
Vitali, Tommasso:
  Chaconne, 48, 89, 136, 179
Vivaldi, Antonio:
  A major Sonata, 136

Walsh, J., 138
Walter, Bruno, 174
Weber, Carl Maria von:
  Rondo Brillante, 220

Webern, Anton, 155
Wieniawski, Henryk, 4, 11
  D minor Concerto, 62
  'Faust' Fantasy, 3, 5
  D major Polonaise, 202–3
  Valse Caprice, 3
Wilhelmj, August, 11, 143; and fingered
  octaves, 73, 81, 145, 146
Wladigeroff, Panchu, 12
Wolf-Ferrari, Ermanno:
  Sonata, 12
Wood, Sir Henry, 6, 175–6

Ysaÿe, Eugène, 6, 8, 11, 20, 124, 136, 201;
  his playing, 173–4, 175, 182
  Solo Sonata No. 3, 191
Ysaÿe, Nicolas, 174
Ysaÿe competition (Brussels 1937), 124